Thomas Hood

Miss Kilmansegg and her precious Leg

A golden Legend

Thomas Hood

Miss Kilmansegg and her precious Leg
A golden Legend

ISBN/EAN: 9783337153915

Printed in Europe, USA, Canada, Australia, Japan

Cover: Foto ©ninafisch / pixelio.de

More available books at **www.hansebooks.com**

Miss Kilmansegg

AND

Her Precious Leg:

A Golden Legend,

BY

THOMAS HOOD.

WITH SIXTY ILLUSTRATIONS
BY
THOS. S. SECCOMBE, Capt. R.A.,
ENGRAVED BY F. JOUBERT.

LONDON: E. MOXON, SON, & CO., DOVER STREET, W.
AND 1, AMEN CORNER, E.C.

CONTENTS.

	PAGE
HER PEDIGREE	1
HER BIRTH	7
HER CHRISTENING	18
HER CHILDHOOD	26
HER EDUCATION	29
HER ACCIDENT	35
HER PRECIOUS LEG	46
HER FAME	51
HER FIRST STEP	57
HER FANCY BALL	60
HER DREAM ...	77
HER COURTSHIP	88
HER HONEYMOON	114
HER MISERY	128
HER LAST WILL	137
HER DEATH ...	140
HER MORAL	148

MISS KILMANSEGG

AND

HER PRECIOUS LEG.

A GOLDEN LEGEND.

Her Pedigree.

To trace the KILMANSEGG pedigree,
To the very root of the family tree,
   Were a task as rash as ridiculous:
Through antediluvian mists as thick
As London fog such a line to pick
Were enough, in truth to puzzle old Nick,—
   Not to name SIR HARRIS NICHOLAS.

It wouldn't require much verbal strain
To trace the KILL MAN, perchance, to CAIN;
   But, waiving all such digressions,
Suffice it, according to family lore,
A Patriarch KILMANSEGG lived of yore,
   Who was famed for his great possessions.

Tradition said he feather'd his nest
Through an Agricultural Interest
  In the Golden Age of Farming;
When golden eggs were laid by the geese,
And COLCHAIN sheep wore a golden fleece,
And golden pippins—the sterling kind
Of HESPERUS—now so hard to find—
  Made Horticulture quite charming!

A Lord of Land, on his own estate,

He lived at a very lively rate,

AND HER PRECIOUS LEG.

But his income would bear carousing ;
Such acres he had of pasture and heath,
With herbage so rich from the ore beneath,
The very ewe's and lambkin's teeth
    Were turn'd into gold by browsing.

He gave, without any extra thrift,
A flock of sheep for a birthday gift
    To each son of his loins, or daughter
And his debts—if debts he had—at will
He liquidated by giving each bill
    A dip in PACTOLIAN water.

'Twas said that even his pigs of lead,
By crossing with some by Midas bred,
    Made a perfect mine of his piggery.
And as for cattle, one yearling bull
Was worth all Smithfield-market full
    Of the Golden Bulls of POPE GREGORY.

The high-bred horses within his stud,
    Like human creatures of birth and blood,

Had their Golden Cups and flagons:
And as for the common husbandry nags,
Their noses were tied in money-bags,
  When they stopp'd with the carts and wagons.

Moreover, he had a Golden Ass,
Sometimes at stall, and sometimes at grass,
  That was worth his own weight in money—
And a golden hive, on a Golden Bank,
Where golden bees, by alchemical prank,
  Gather'd gold instead of honey.

AND HER PRECIOUS LEG.

Gold! and gold! and gold without end!
He had gold to lay by, and gold to spend,
Gold to give, and gold to lend,
 And reversions of gold in futuro.
In wealth the family revell'd and roll'd,
Himself and wife and sons so bold;—
 "O bella eta del oro!"

Such was the tale of the KILMANSEGG Kin,
In golden text on a vellum skin,

Though certain people would wink and grin,

And declare the whole story a parable —
That the Ancestor rich was one JACOB GHRIMES,
Who held a long lease, in prosperous times,
   Of acres, pasture and arable.

That as money makes money, his golden bees
Where the Five per Cents., or which you please,
   When his cash was more than plenty—
That the golden cups were racing affairs;
And his daughters, who sang Italian airs,
   Had their golden harps of CLEMENTI.

That the Golden Ass, or Golden Bull,
Was ENGLISH JOHN, with his pockets full,
   Then at war by land and water:
While beef, and mutton, and other meat,
Were almost as dear as money to eat,
And Farmers reaped Golden Harvests of wheat
   At the Lord knows what per quarter!

Her Birth.

What different dooms our birthdays bring!
For instance, one little manikin thing
　Survives to wear many a wrinkle;
While death forbids another to wake,
And a son that it took nine moons to make
　Expires without even a twinkle!

　　Into this world we come like ships,
　　Launch'd from the docks, and stocks, and slips,
　　　For fortune fair or fatal;
　　And one little craft is cast away
　　In its very first trip in Babbicome Bay,
　　　While another rides safe at Port Natal.

MISS KILMANSEGG

What different lots our stars accord!
This babe to be hail'd and woo'd as a Lord!

AND HER PRECIOUS LEG.

And that to be shunn'd like a leper!
One, to the world's wine, honey, and corn,
Another, like a Colchester native, born
    To its vinegar, only, and pepper.

One is litter'd under a roof
Neither wind nor water proof,—
    That's the prose of Love in a Cottage,—
A puny, naked, shivering wretch,
The whole of whose birthright would not fetch,
Though ROBINS himself drew up the sketch,
    The bid of "a mess of pottage."

Born of FORTUNATUS'S kin,
Another comes tenderly usher'd in
    To a prospect all bright and burnish'd:
No tenant he for life's back slums—
He comes to the world as a gentleman comes
    To a lodging ready furnish'd.

And the other sex—the tender—the fair—
What wide reverses of fate are there!
Whilst MARGARET, charm'd by the Bulbul rare,

In a garden of Gul reposes—
Poor Peggy hawks nosegays from street to street
Till—think of that, who find life so sweet —
She hates the smell of roses.

AND HER PRECIOUS LEG.

Not so with the infant KILMANSEGG!
She was not born to steal or beg,
  Or gather cresses in ditches;
To plait the straw or bind the shoe,
Or sit all day to hem and sew,
As females must,—and not a few—
  To fill their insides with stitches

MISS KILMANSEGG

She was not doom'd, for bread to eat,
To be put to her hands as well as her feet
   To carry home linen from mangles—
Or heavy hearted, and weary-limb'd,
To dance on a rope in a jacket trimm'd
   With as many blows as spangles.

She was one of those who by Fortune's boon
Are born, as they say, with a silver spoon
   In her mouth, not a wooden ladle:
To speak according to poet's wont,
Plutus as sponsor stood at her font,
   And Midas rock'd the cradle.

At her first debut she found her head
On a pillow of down, in a downy bed,
   With a damask canopy over,
For although, by the vulgar popular saw
All mothers are said to be "in the straw,"
   Some children are born in clover.

Her very first draught of vital air,
It was not the common chameleon fare
   Of plebeian lungs and noses,—
     No—her earliest sniff
     Of this world was a whiff
   Of the genuine Otto of Roses!

AND HER PRECIOUS LEG.

When she saw the light, it was no mere ray
Of that light so common—so everyday—
   That the sun each morning launches—
But six wax tapers dazzled her eyes,
From a thing—a gooseberry bush for size—
   With a golden stem and branches.

She was born exactly at half-past two,
As witness'd a time-piece in or-molu
   That stood on a marble table—
Showing at once the time of day,
And a team of Gildings running away
   As fast as they were able,
With a golden God, with a golden Star,
And a golden Spear, in a golden Car,
   According to Grecian fable.

Like other babes, at her birth she cried;
Which made a sensation far and wide,
   Ay, for twenty miles around her;
For though to the ear 'twas nothing more
Than an infant's squall, it was really the roar
   Of a Fifty-thousand Pounder!
     It shook the next heir
     In his library chair,
   And made him cry, "Confound her!"

MISS KILMANSEGG

Of signs and omens there was no dearth,
Any more than at OWEN GLENDOWER'S birth,
  Or the advent of other great people:
    Two bullocks dropp'd dead,
    As if knock'd on the head,
    And barrels of stout
    And ale ran about,
And the village-bells such a peal rang out,
  That they crack'd the village-steeple.

In no time at all, like mushroom spawn,
Tables sprang up all over the lawn;
  Not furnish'd scantly or shabbily,
    But on scale as vast
    As that huge repast,
    With its loads and cargoes
    Of drink and botargoes,
  At the birth of the Babe in Rabelais.

Hundreds of men were turn'd into beasts,
Like the guests at CIRCE'S horrible feasts,
  By the magic of ale and cider:
And each country lass, and each country lad,
Began to caper and dance like mad,
And ev'n some old ones appear'd to have had
  A bite from the Naples Spider.

AND HER PRECIOUS LEG.

Then as night came on,
It had scared KING JOHN,
Who considered such signs not risible,
To have seen the maroons,
And the whirling moons,
And the serpents of flame,
And wheels of the same,
That according to some were "whizzable"

MISS KILMANSEGG

Oh, happy HOPE of the KILMANSEGGS!
Thrice happy in head, and body, and legs,
　That her parents had such full pockets!
For had she been born of Want and Thrift,
For care and nursing all adrift,
It's ten to one she had had to make shift
　With rickets instead of rockets!

And how was the precious baby drest?
In a robe of the East, with lace of the West,
　Like one of CRŒSUS'S issue—
　　Her best bibs were made
　　Of rich gold brocade,
　And the others of silver tissue.

And when the BABY inclined to nap
She was lull'd on a GROS DE NAPLES lap,
By a nurse in a modish PARIS cap,
　Of notions so exalted,
She drank nothing lower than CURACOA,
MARASCHINO, or pink NOYAU,
　And on principle never malted.

From a golden boat, with a golden spoon,
The babe was fed night, morning, and noon;

AND HER PRECIOUS LEG.

And altho' the tale seems fabulous,
'Tis said her tops and bottoms were gilt,
Like the oats in that Stable-yard Palace built
For the horse of HELIOGABALUS.

And when she took to squall and kick—
For pain will wring, and pins will prick,
　E'en the wealthiest nabob's daughter—
They gave her no vulgar DALBY or gin,
But a liquor with leaf of gold therein,
　Videlicet,—DANTZIC WATER.

In short she was born, and bred, and nurst,
And drest in the best from the very first,
　To please the genteelest censor—
And then, as soon as strength would allow
Was vaccinated, as babes are now,
With virus ta'en from the best bred cow
　Of Lord ALTHORPE's—now EARL SPENCER.

Her Christening.

Though SHAKESPEARE asks us, "What's in a name?"
(As if cognomens were much the same),
   There's really a very great scope in it.
A name?—why, wasn't there DOCTOR DODD,
That servant at once of MAMMON and GOD,
Who found four thousand pounds and odd,
   A prison—a cart—and a rope in it?

A name?—if the party had a voice,
What mortal would be a BUGG by choice?
As a HOGG, a GRUBB, or a CHUBB rejoice?
   Or any such nauseous blazon?
Not to mention many a vulgar name,
That would make a door-plate blush for shame,
   If door-plates were not so brazen!

A name?—it has more than nominal worth,
And belongs to good or bad luck at birth—
   As dames of a certain degree know.

AND HER PRECIOUS LEG.

In spite of his PAGE'S hat and hose,
His PAGE'S jacket, and buttons in rows,
BOB only sounds like a page in prose
    Till turn'd into RUPERTINO.

Now to christen the infant KILMANSEGG,
For days and days it was quite a plague,
    To hunt the list in the LEXICON:
And scores were tried, like coin, by the ring,
Ere names were found just the proper thing
    For a minor rich as a MEXICAN.

Then cards were sent the presence to beg
Of all the kin of KILMANSEGG,
    White, yellow, and brown relations:
Brothers, Wardens of City Halls,
And Uncles—rich as three Golden Balls
    From taking pledges of nations.

Nephews, whom Fortune seem'd to bewitch,
    Rising in life like rockets—
Nieces, whose dowries knew no hitch—
Aunts, as certain of dying rich
    As candles in golden sockets—

MISS KILMANSEGG

Cousins German and Cousins' sons,
All thriving and opulent—some had tons
   Of Kentish hops in their pockets!

For money had stuck to the race through life
(As it did to the bushel when cash so rife
Posed ALI BABA'S brother's wife)—
   And down to the Cousins and Coz-lings,
The fortunate brood of the KILMANSEGGS.
As if they had come out of golden eggs,
   Were all as wealthy as " GOSLINGS."

It would fill a Court Gazette to name
What East and West End people came
   To the rite of Christianity:
The lofty Lord, and titled Dame,
   All di'monds, plumes, and urbanity:
His Lordship the May'r with his golden chain,
And two Gold Sticks and the Sheriffs twain,
Nine foreign Counts, and other great men
With orders and stars, to help " M. or N."
   To renounce all pomp and vanity.

To paint the maternal Kilmansegg
The pen of an Eastern poet would beg,
   And need an elaborate sonnet;

AND HER PRECIOUS LEG.

How she sparkled with gems whenever she stirr'd,
And her head niddle-noddled at every word,
And seem'd so happy, a Paradise bird
   Had nidificated upon it.

And Sir Jacob the Father strutted and bow'd,
And smiled to himself, and laugh'd aloud,
   To think of his heiress and daughter—
And then in his pockets he made a grope,
And then in the fulness of joy and hope,
Seem'd washing his hands with invisible soap
   In imperceptible water.

He had roll'd in money like pigs in mud,
Till it seem'd to have enter'd into his blood
  By some occult projection:
And his cheeks instead of a healthy hue,
As yellow as any guinea grew,
Making the common phrase seem true,
  About a rich complexion.

And now came the nurse, and during a pause,
Her dead-leaf satin would fitly cause
  A very autumnal rustle—
So full of figure, so full of fuss,
As she carried about the babe to buss,
  She seem'd to be nothing but bustle.

A wealthy NABOB was Godpapa,
And an Indian BEGUM was Godmamma,
  Whose jewels a QUEEN might covet—
And the Priest was a VICAR, and DEAN withal
Of that Temple we see with a Golden Ball,
  And a Golden Cross above it.

The Font was a bowl of American gold,

AND HER PRECIOUS LEG.

Won by RALEIGH in days of old,
In spite of Spanish bravado;

And the Book of Pray'r was so overrun
With gilt devices, it shone in the sun
Like a copy—a presentation one—
   Of Humboldt's "El Dorado."

Gold! and gold! and nothing but gold!
The same auriferous shine behold
   Wherever the eye could settle!
On the walls—the sideboard—the ceiling—sky—
On the gorgeous footmen standing by,
In coats to delight a miner's eye
   With seams of the precious metal.

Gold! and gold! and besides the gold,
The very robe of the infant told
A tale of wealth in every fold,
   It lapp'd her like a vapour!
So fine! so thin! the mind at a loss
Could compare it to nothing except a cross
   Of cobweb with bank-note paper.

Then her pearls—'twas a perfect sight, forsooth,
To see them, like "the dew of her youth,"
   In such a plentiful sprinkle.
Meanwhile, the Vicar read through the form,
And gave her another, not overwarm,
   That made her little eyes twinkle.

AND HER PRECIOUS LEG.

Then the babe was cross'd and bless'd amain;
But instead of the KATE, or ANN, or JANE,
 Which the humbler female endorses—
Instead of one name, as some people prefix,
Kilmansegg went at the tails of six,
 Like a carriage of state with its horses.

Oh, then the kisses she got and hugs!
The golden mugs and the golden jugs
 That lent fresh rays to the midges!
The golden knives, and the golden spoons,
The gems that sparkled like fairy boons,
It was one of the KILMANSEGG'S own saloons,
 But look'd like RUNDELL and BRIDGE'S!

Gold! and gold! the new and the old!
The company ate and drank from gold,
 They revell'd, they sung, and were merry;
And one of the Gold Sticks rose from his chair
And toasted "the Lass with the golden hair,"
 In a bumper of Golden Sherry.

Gold! still gold! it rain'd on the nurse,
Who, unlike Danae, was none the worse;
 There was nothing but guineas glistening!
 Fifty were given to Doctor James,

For calling the little Baby names,
And for saying, Amen!
The Clerk had ten,
And that was the end of the Christening.

Her Childhood.

Our youth! our childhood! that spring of springs!
'Tis surely one of the blessedest things
   That nature ever invented!
When the rich are wealthy beyond their wealth,
And the poor are rich in spirits and health,
And all with their lots contented!

There's little Phelim, he sings like a thrush,
In the self-same pair of patchwork plush,
   With the self-same empty pockets,
That tempted his daddy so often to cut
His throat, or jump into the water-butt—
But what cares Phelim? an empty nut
   Would sooner bring tears to their sockets.

Give him a collar without a shirt,
That's the Irish linen for shirt,

AND HER PRECIOUS LEG.

And a slice of bread, with a taste of dirt,
    That's Poverty's Irish butter,
And what does he lack to make him blest?
Some oyster-shells, or a sparrow's nest,
    A candle-end and a gutter.

But to leave the happy Phelim alone,
Gnawing, perchance, a marrowless bone,
    For which no dog would quarrel—
Turn we to little Miss KILMANSEGG,
Cutting her first little toothy-peg
    With a fifty-guinea coral—

MISS KILMANSEGG

A peg upon which
About poor and rich
Reflection might hang a moral.

Born in wealth, and wealthily nursed,
Capp'd, papp'd, napp'd, and lapp'd from the first
  On the knees of Prodigality,
Her childhood was one eternal round
Of the game of going on Tidler's ground
  Picking up gold—in reality.

With extempore carts she never play'd,
Or the odds and ends of a Tinker's trade,
Or little dirt pies and puddings made,
  Like children happy and squalid;
The very puppet she had to pet,
Like a bait for the "NIX MY DOLLY" set,
  Was a Dolly of gold—and solid!

Gold! and gold! 'twas the burden still!
To gain the Heiress's early goodwill
  There was much corruption and bribery—
The yearly cost of her golden toys
Would have given half London's Charity Boys
And Charity Girls the annual joys
  Of a holiday dinner at Highbury.

AND HER PRECIOUS LEG.

Bon-bons she ate from the gilt cornet ;
And gilded queens on St. Bartlemy's day ;
   Till her fancy was tinged by her presents—
And first a Goldfinch excited her wish,
Then a spherical bowl with its Golden fish,
   And then two Golden Pheasants.

Nay, once she squall'd and scream'd like wild—
And it shows how the bias we give to a child
   Is a thing most weighty and solemn :—
But whence was wonder or blame to spring
If little Miss K.—after such a swing—
Made a dust for the flaming gilded thing
   On the top of the Fish Street column?

Her Education.

According to metaphysical creed,
To the earliest books that children read
   For much good or much bad they are debtors—
But before with their A B C they start,
There are things in morals, as well as art,
That play a very important part—
   " Impressions before the letters."

Dame Education begins the pile,
Mayhap in the graceful Corinthian style,
  But alas for the elevation!
If the Lady's maid or Gossip the Nurse
With a load of rubbish, or something worse,
  Have made a rotten foundation.

Even thus with little Miss KILMANSEGG,
Before she learnt her E for Egg,
  Ere her Governess came, or her masters—
Teachers of quite a different kind
Had "cramm'd" her beforehand, and put her mind
  In a go-cart on golden castors.

Long before her A B and C,
They had taught her by heart her L. S. D.
  And as how she was born a great Heiress:
And as sure as London is built of bricks,
My Lord would ask her the day to fix,
To ride in a fine gilt coach and six,
  Like Her Worship the Lady May'ress.

Instead of stories from Edgeworth's page,
The true golden lore for our golden age,
  Or lessons from Barbauld and Trimmer,
Teaching the worth of Virtue and Health,

AND HER PRECIOUS LEG.

All that she knew was the Virtue of Wealth,
Provided by vulgar nursery stealth
  With a Book of Leaf Gold for a Primer.

The very metal of merit they told,
And praised her for being as "good as gold!
  Till she grew as a peacock haughty;
Of money they talk'd the whole day round,
And weigh'd dessert like grapes by the pound,
Till she had an idea from the very sound
  That people with nought were naughty.

MISS KILMANSEGG

They praised—poor children with nothing at all
Lord! how you twaddle and waddle and squall
   Like common-bred geese and ganders!
What sad little bad little figures you make
To the rich Miss K., whose plainest seed-cake
   Was stuff'd with corianders!

They praised her falls, as well as her walk,
Flatterers make cream cheese of chalk,
They praised—how they praised—her very small talk,
   As if it fell from a Solon;
Or the girl who at each pretty phrase let drop
A ruby comma, or pearl full-stop,
   Or an emerald semi-colon.

They praised her spirit, and now and then,
The Nurse brought her own little "nevy" Ben,
   To play with the future May'ress,
And when he got raps, and taps, and slaps,
Scratches, and pinches, snips, and snaps,
   As if from a Tigress, or Bearess,
They told him how Lords would court that hand,
And always gave him to understand,
     While he rubb'd, poor soul,
     His carrotty poll,
That his hair had been pull'd by "a Hairess."

AND HER PRECIOUS LEG.

Such were the lessons from maid and nurse,
A Governess help'd to make still worse,
Giving an appetite so perverse
   Fresh diet whereon to batten—
Beginning with A B C to hold
Like a royal playbill printed in gold
   On a square of pearl-white satin.

The books to teach the verbs and nouns,
And those about countries, cities, and towns,
Instead of their sober drabs and browns,
   Were in crimson silk, with gilt edges;—
Her BUTLER, and ENFIELD, and ENTICK—in short
Her "Early Lessons" of every sort,
   Look'd like Souvenirs, Keepsakes, and Pledges.

Old JOHNSON shone out in as fine array
As he did one night when he went to the play;
CHAMBAUD like a beau of KING CHARLES'S day—
   LINDLEY MURRAY in like conditions—
Each weary, unwelcome, irksome task,
Appear'd in a fancy dress and a mask—
If you wish for similar copies, ask
   For HOWELL and JAMES'S Editions.

Novels she read to amuse her mind,
But always the affluent matchmaking kind

That ends with Promessi Sposi,
And a father-in-law so wealthy and grand,
He could give check-mate to Coutts in the Strand;
   So, along with a ring and posy,
He endows the Bride with Golconda off hand,
   And gives the Groom Potosi.

Plays she perused—but she liked the best
Those comedy gentlefolks always possess'd
   Of fortunes so truly romantic—
Of money so ready that right or wrong
It always is ready to go for a song,
Throwing it, going it, pitching it strong—
They ought to have purses as green and long
   As the cucumber call'd the Gigantic.

The Eastern Tales she loved for the sake
Of the Purse of Oriental make,
   And the thousand pieces they put in it—
But Pastoral scenes on her heart fell cold,
For Nature with her had lost its hold,
No field but the Field of the Cloth of Gold
   Would ever have caught her foot in it.

What more? She learnt to sing and dance,
To sit on a horse, although he should prance,
And to speak a French not spoken in France

AND HER PRECIOUS LEG.

Any more than at Babel's building—
And she painted shells, and flowers, and Turks,
But her great delight was in Fancy Works
  That are done with gold or gilding.

Gold! still Gold!—the bright and the dead,
With golden beads, and gold lace, and gold thread
She work'd in gold as if for her bread;
  The metal had so undermined her,
Gold ran in her thoughts and fill'd her brain,
She was golden headed as Peter's cane
  With which he walk'd behind her.

Her Accident.

The horse that carried Miss KILMANSEGG,
And a better never lifted leg,
  Was a very rich bay, call'd Banker—
A horse of a breed and a mettle so rare,—

By Bullion out of an Ingot mare,—
That for action, the best of figures, and air,
  It made many good judges hanker.

AND HER PRECIOUS LEG.

And when she took a ride in the Park,
Equestrian Lord, or pedestrian Clerk,
   Was thrown in an amorous fever,
To see the Heiress how well she sat,
With her groom behind her, Bob or Nat,
In green, half smother'd with gold, and a hat
   With more gold lace than beaver.

And then when Banker obtain'd a pat,
To see how he arch'd his neck at that!
   He snorted with pride and pleasure!
Like the Steed in the fable so lofty and grand,
Who gave the poor Ass to understand,
That he didn't carry a bag of sand,
   But a burden of golden treasure.

A load of treasure?—alas! alas!
Had her horse but been fed upon English grass,
   And shelter'd in Yorkshire spinneys,
Had he scour'd the sand with the Desert Ass,
   Or where the American whinnies—
But a hunter from Erin's turf and gorse,
A regular thorough-bred Irish horse,
Why, he ran away as a matter of course,
   With a girl worth her weight in guineas!

MISS KILMANSEGG

Mayhap 'tis the trick of such pamper'd nags
To shy at the sight of a beggar in rags,—
But away, like the bolt of a rabbit,—

Away went the horse in the madness of fright,
And away went the horsewoman mocking the sight—
Was yonder blue flash a flash of blue light,
    Or only the skirt of her habit?

Away she flies, with the groom behind,—
It looks like a race of the Calmuck kind,
    When Hymen himself is the starter:

AND HER PRECIOUS LEG.

And the Maid rides first in the fourfooted strife,
Riding, striding, as if for her life,
While the Lover rides after to catch him a wife,
   Although it's catching a Tartar.

But the Groom has lost his glittering hat!
Though he does not sigh and pull up for that—
Alas! his horse is a tit for Tat
   To sell to a very low bidder—
His wind is ruin'd, his shoulder is sprung,
Things, though a horse be handsome and young,
   A purchaser will consider.

But still flies the Heiress through stones and dust,
O, for a fall, if fall she must,
   On the gentle lap of Flora!
But still, thank Heaven! she clings to her seat—
Away! away! she could ride a dead heat
With the Dead who ride so fast and fleet,
   In the Ballad of Leonora!

Away she gallops,—its awful work,
It's faster than Turpin's ride to York,
   On Bess that notable clipper!

She has circled the Ring—she crosses the Park!
Mazeppa, although he was stripped so stark,
 Mazeppa couldn't outstrip her!

The fields seem running away with the folks!
The Elms are having a race for the Oaks!
 At a pace that all jockeys disparages!

AND HER PRECIOUS LEG.

All, all is racing! the Serpentine
Seems rushing past like the "arrowy Rhine."
The houses have got on a railway line,
    And are off like the first-class carriages!

She'll lose her life! she is losing her breath!
A cruel chase, she is chasing Death,
    As female shriekings forewarn her;
And now—as gratis as blood of GUELPH—
She clears that gate, which has clear'd itself
    Since then, at Hyde Park Corner!

Alas! for the hope of the KILMANSEGGS!
For her head, her brains, her body, and legs,
    Her life's not worth a copper!
        Willy-nilly,
        In Piccadilly,
    A hundred hearts turn sick and chilly,
    A hundred voices cry, "Stop her!"
And one old gentleman stares and stands,
Shakes his head and lifts his hands,
    And says "How very improper!"

On and on!—what a perilous run!
The iron rails seem all mingling in one,
  To shut out the Green Park scenery!
And now the Cellar its dangers reveals,
She shudders—she shrieks—she's doom'd, she feels,
To be torn by powers of horses and wheels,
  Like a spinner by steam machinery!

Sick with horror she shuts her eyes,
But the very stones seem uttering cries,

AND HER PRECIOUS LEG.

As they did to that Persian daughter,
When she climb'd up the steep vociferous hill,
   Her little silver flagon to fill
     With the magical Golden Water!

     " Batter her! shatter her!
     Throw and scatter her!"
Shouts each stony-hearted chatterer!
     " Dash at the heavy Dover!
Spill her! kill her! tear and tatter her!
Smash her! crash her!" (the stones didn't flatter her!)
" Kick her brains out! let her blood spatter her!
     Roll on her over and over!"

For so she gather'd the awful sense
Of the street in its past unmacadamized tense,
   As the wild horse overran it,—
His four heels making the clatter of six,
Like a Devil's tattoo, play'd with iron sticks
   On a kettle-drum of granite.

On! still on! she's dazzled with hints
Of oranges, ribbons, and colour'd prints,
A Kaleidoscope jumble of shapes and tints,
   And human faces all flashing,
Bright and brief as the sparks from the flints,
   That the desperate hoof keeps dashing!

On and on! still frightfully fast!
DOVER STREET, Bond street, all are past!

But—yes—no—yes!—they're down at last!
The FURIES and FATES have found them!
Down they go with a sparkle and crash,
Like a Bark that's struck by the lightning flash—
There's a shriek—and a sob—
And the dense dark mob
Like a billow closes around them!

AND HER PRECIOUS LEG.

"She breathes!"
"She don't!"
"She'll recover!"
"She won't!"
"She's stirring! she's living, by NEMESIS!"
Gold! still Gold! on counter and shelf!
Golden dishes as plenty as delf;
Miss Kilmansegg's coming again to herself
    On an opulent Goldsmith's premises!

Gold! fine Gold!—both yellow and red,
Beaten, and molten—polish'd, and dead—
To see the gold with profusion spread
    In all forms of its manufacture!
But what avails gold to Miss KILMANSEGG,
When the femoral bone of her dexter leg
    Has met with a compound fracture?

Gold may soothe Adversity's smart;
Nay, help to bind up a broken heart;
But to try it on any other part
    Were as certain a disappointment,
As if one should rub the dish and plate,
Taken out of a Staffordshire crate—
In the hope of a Golden Service of State—
    With Singleton's "Golden Ointment."

Her Precious Leg.

"As the twig is bent, the tree's inclined,"
Is an adage often recall'd to mind,
   Referring to juvenile bias;
And never so well is the verity seen,
As when to the weak warp'd side we lean,
   While Life's tempests and hurricanes try us.

Even thus with Miss K. and her broken limb;
By a very, very remarkable whim,
   She showed her early tuition;
While the buds of character came into blow
With a certain tinge that served to show
The nursery culture long ago,
   As the graft is known by fruition!

AND HER PRECIOUS LEG.

For the King's Physician, who nursed the case,
His verdict gave with an awful face,
    And three others concurr'd to egg it;
That the Patient to give old DEATH the slip,
Like the Pope, instead of a personal trip,
    Must send her Leg as a Legate.

The limb was doom'd—it couldn't be saved!
And like other people the patient behaved,
Nay, bravely that cruel parting braved,

Which makes some persons so falter,
They rather would part, without a groan,
With the flesh of their flesh, or bone of their bone
    They obtain'd at St. George's altar.

But when it came to fitting the stump
With a proxy limb—then flatly and plump
    She spoke, in the spirit olden;
She couldn't—she shouldn't—she wouldn't have wood!
Nor a leg of cork, if she never stood,
And she swore an oath, or something as good,
    The proxy limb should be golden!

A wooden leg! what, a sort of peg,
    For your common Jockeys and Jennies!
No, no, her mother might worry and plague—
Weep, go down on her knees, and beg,
But nothing would move Miss KILMANSEGG!
She could—she would have a Golden Leg,
    If it cost ten thousand guineas!

Wood indeed, in Forest or Park,
With its sylvan honours and feudal bark,
    Is an aristocratic article:
But split and sawn, and hack'd about town,

AND HER PRECIOUS LEG.

Serving all needs of pauper or clown,
Trod on! stagger'd on! Wood cut down
   Is vulgar—fibre and particle!

And Cork!—when the noble Cork tree shades
A lovely group of Castilian maids,
   'Tis a thing for a song or sonnet!—
But cork, as it stops the bottle of gin,
Or bungs the beer—the small beer—in,
It pierced her heart like a corking-pin,
   To think of standing upon it!

MISS KILMANSEGG

A Leg of Gold—solid gold throughout,
Nothing else, whether slim or stout,
　　Should ever support her, God willing!
She must—she could—she would have her whim,
Her father, she turn'd a deaf ear to him—
　　He might kill her—she didn't mind killing!
He was welcome to cut off her other limb—
　　He might cut her all off with a shilling!

All other promised gifts were in vain,
Golden Girdle, or Golden Chain,
She writhed with impatience more than pain,
　　And utter'd "pshaws!" and "pishes!"
But a Leg of Gold as she lay in bed,
It danced before her—it ran in her head!
　　It jump'd with her dearest wishes!

"Gold—gold—gold! Oh, let it be gold!"
Asleep or awake that tale she told,
　　And when she grew delirious:
Till her parents resolved to grant her wish,
If they melted down plate, and goblet, and dish,
　　The case was getting so serious.

So a Leg was made in a comely mould,
Of Gold, fine virgin glittering gold,
　　As solid as man could make it—

AND HER PRECIOUS LEG.

Solid in foot, and calf, and shank;
A prodigious sum of money it sank;
In fact 'twas a branch of the family Bank,
    And no easy matter to break it.

All sterling metal—not half-and-half,
The Goldsmith's mark was stamp'd on the calf—
    'Twas pure as from Mexican barter!
And to make it more costly, just over the knee,
Where another ligature used to be,
Was a circle of jewels, worth shillings to see,
    A new-fangled Badge of the Garter!

'Twas a splendid, brilliant, beautiful leg,
Fit for the Court of Scander-Beg,
That Precious Leg of Miss KILMANSEGG!
    For, thanks to parental bounty,
Secure from Mortification's touch,
She stood on a Member that cost as much
    As a Member for all the County!

Her Fame.

To gratify stern ambition's whims,
What hundreds and thousands of precious limbs
    On a field of battle we scatter!

Sever'd by sword, or bullet, or saw,
Off they go, all bleeding and raw,
But the public seems to get the lock-jaw,
   So little is said of the matter!

Legs, the tightest that ever were seen,
The tightest, the lightest that danced on the green,
   .Cutting capers to sweet KITTY CLOVER;
Shatter'd, scatter'd, cut, and bowl'd down,
Off they go, worse off for renown,
A line in the *Times*, or a talk about town,
   Than the leg that a fly runs over!

AND HER PRECIOUS LEG.

But the Precious Leg of Miss KILMANSEGG,
That gowden, goolden, golden leg,
   Was the theme of all conversation!
Had it been a Pillar of Church and State,
Or a prop to support the whole Dead Weight,
It could not have furnish'd more debate
   To the heads and tails of the nation!

East and West, and north and south,
Though useless for either hunger or drouth,—
The Leg was in everybody's mouth,
   To use a poetical figure,
Rumour, in taking her ravenous swim,
Saw, and seized on the tempting limb,
   Like a shark on the leg of a nigger.

Wilful murder fell very dead;
Debates in the House were hardly read;
In vain the Police Reports were fed
   With Irish riots and rumpuses—
The Leg! the Leg! was the great event,
Through every circle in life it went,
   Like the leg of a pair of compasses.

The last new novel seem'd tame and flat,
The Leg, a novelty newer than that,

AND HER PRECIOUS LEG.

Had tripp'd up the heels of Fiction!
It Burked the very essays of Burke,
And, alas! how Wealth over Wit plays the Turk!
As a regular piece of goldsmith's work,
    Got the better of Goldsmith's diction.

"A leg of gold! what of solid gold?"
Cried rich and poor, and young and old,—
    And Master and Miss and Madam—
'Twas the talk of 'Change—the Alley—the Bank—
And with men of scientific rank,

It made as much stir as the fossil shank
    Of a Lizard coeval with Adam!

Of course with Greenwich and Chelsea elves,
Men who had lost a limb themselves,
   Its interest did not dwindle—
But Bill, and Ben, and Jack, and Tom
Could hardly have spun more yarns therefrom,
   If the leg had been a spindle.

Meanwhile the story went to and fro,
Till, gathering like the ball of snow,
By the time it got to Stratford-le-Bow,
   Through Exaggeration's touches,
The Heiress and Hope of the KILMANSEGGS
Was propp'd on two fine Golden Legs,
   And a pair of Golden Crutches!

Never had Leg so great a run!
'Twas the "go" and the "Kick" thrown into one!
The mode—the new thing under the sun,
   The rage—the fancy—the passion!
Bonnets were named, and hats were worn,
A la Golden Leg instead of Leghorn,
      And stockings and shoes,
         Of golden hues,
   Took the lead in walks of fashion!

AND HER PRECIOUS LEG.

The Golden Leg had a vast career,
It was sung and danced—and to show how near
   Low Folly to lofty approaches,
Down to society's very dregs,
The Belles of Wapping wore " KILMANSEGGS,"
And St. Giles's Beaux sported Golden Legs
   In their pinchbeck pins and brooches!

Her First Step.

Supposing the Trunk and Limbs of Man
Shared, on the allegorical plan,
   By the Passions that mark Humanity,
Whichever might claim the head, or heart,
The stomach, or any other part,
   The Legs would be seized by Vanity.

There's BARDUS, a six-foot column of fop,
A lighthouse without any light atop,
   Whose height would attract beholders,
If he had not lost some inches clear
By looking down at his kerseymere,
Ogling the limbs he holds so dear,
   Till he got a stoop in his shoulders.

MISS KILMANSEGG

Talk of Art, of Science, or Books,
And down go the everlasting looks,
　To his crural beauties so wedded!
Try him, wherever you will, you find
His mind in his legs, and his legs in his mind,
All prongs and folly—in short a kind
　Of fork—that is fiddle-headed.

What wonder, then, if Miss KILMANSEGG,
With a splendid, brilliant, beautiful leg,
Fit for the court of Scander-Beg,
Disdain'd to hide it like Joan or Meg,
　In petticoats stuff'd or quilted?
Not she! 'twas her convalescent whim
To dazzle the world with her precious limb,—
　Nay, to go a little high-kilted.

So cards were sent for that sort of mob
Where Tartars and Africans hob-and-nob,
And the Cherokee talks of his cab and cob
　To Polish or Lapland lovers—
Cards like that hieroglyphical call
To a geographical Fancy Ball
　On the recent Post Office covers.

For if Lion-hunters—and great ones too—
Would mob a savage from Latakoo,
Or squeeze for a glimpse of Prince LEE BOO,
 That unfortunate Sandwich scion—
Hundreds of first-rate people, no doubt,
Would gladly, madly, rush to a rout,
 That promised a Golden Lion!

Her Fancy Ball.

Of all the spirits of evil fame
That hurt the soul or injure the frame,
   And poison what's honest and hearty,

There's none more needs a Mathew to preach
A cooling, antiphlogistic speech,

AND HER PRECIOUS LEG.

To praise and enforce
A temperate course,
Than the Evil Spirit of Party.

Go to the House of Commons, or Lords,
And they seem to be busy with simple words
  In their popular sense or pedantic—
But, alas! with their cheers, and sneers, and jeers,
They're really busy, whatever appears,
Putting peas in each other's ears,
  To drive their enemies frantic!

Thus Tories love to worry the Whigs,
Who treat them in turn like Schwalbach pigs.
Giving them lashes, thrashes, and digs,
  With their writhing and pain delighted—
But after all that's said, and more,
The malice and spite of Party are poor
To the malice and spite of a party next door,
  To a party not invited.

On with the cap and out with the light,
Weariness bids the world good night,

MISS KILMANSEGG

At least for the usual season;
But hark! a clatter of horses' heels!
And Sleep and Silence are broken on wheels,
Like Wilful Murder and Treason!

Another crash—and the carriage goes—
Again poor Weariness seeks the repose
　That Nature demands, imperious;
But Echo takes up the burden now,
With a rattling chorus of row-de-dow-dow,
Till Silence herself seems making a row,
　Like a Quaker gone delirious!

'Tis night—a winter night—and the stars
Are shining like winkin'—Venus and Mars
Are rolling along in their golden cars
　Through the sky's serene expansion—
But vainly the stars dispense their rays,
Venus and Mars are lost in the blaze
　Of the KILMANSEGG's luminous mansion!

Up jumps Fear in a terrible fright!
His bedchamber windows look so bright,—

AND HER PRECIOUS LEG.

With light all the Square is glutted!
Up he jumps, like a sole from the pan,
And a tremor sickens his inward man,
For he feels as only a gentleman can,
    Who thinks he's being "gutted."

Again Fears settles, all snug and warm;
But only to dream of a dreadful storm
    From Autumn's sulphurous locker;
But the only electrical body that falls,
Wears a negative coat, and positive smalls,
And draws the peal that so appals
    From the KILMANSEGGS' brazen knocker!

'Tis Curiosity's benefit night—
And perchance 'tis the English-Second-Sight,
    But whatever it be, so be it—
As the friends and guests of Miss KILMANSEGG
Crowd in to look at her Golden Leg,
        As many more
        Mob round the door,
    To see them going to see it!

MISS KILMANSEGG

AND HER PRECIOUS LEG.

In they go—in jackets, and cloaks,
Plumes, and bonnets, turbans, and toques,
   As if to a Congress of Nations:
Greeks and Malays, with daggers and dirks,
Spaniards, Jews, Chinese, and Turks—
Some like original foreign works,
   But mostly like bad translations.

In they go, and to work like a pack,
Iuan, Moses, and Shacabac,
Tom, and Jerry, and Springheel'd Jack,
   For some of low fancy are lovers—
Skirting, zigzagging, casting about,
Here and there, and in and out,
With a crush, and a rush, for a full-bodied rout
   In one of the stiffest of covers.

In they went, and hunted about,
Open mouth'd like chub and trout,
And some with the upper lip thrust out,
   Like that fish for routing, a barbel—
While Sir Jacob stood to welcome the crowd,
And rubb'd his hands, and smiled aloud,
And bow'd, and bow'd, and bow'd, and bow'd,
   Like a man who is sawing marble.

MISS KILMANSEGG

AND HER PRECIOUS LEG.

For Princes were there, and Noble Peers;
Dukes descended from Norman spears;
Earls that dated from early years;
   And Lords in vast variety—
Besides the Gentry both new and old—
For people who stand on legs of gold,
   Are sure to stand well with society.

"But where—where—where?" with one accord
Cried Moses and Mufti, Jack and my Lord,
   Wang-Fong and Il Bondocani—
When slow, and heavy, and dead as a dump,
   They heard a foot begin to stump,
      Thump! lump!
      Lump! thump!
   Like the Spectre in "Don Giovanni!"

And lo! the Heiress, Miss KILMANSEGG,
With her splendid, brilliant, beautiful leg,
   In the garb of a Goddess olden—
Like chaste Diana going to hunt,
With a golden spear—which of course was blunt,
And a tunic loop'd up to a gem in front,
   To show the Leg that was Golden!

Gold! still gold! her Crescent behold,
   That should be silver, but would be gold;
   And her robe's auriferous spangles!

Her golden stomacher—how she would melt!
Her golden quiver, and golden belt,
  Where a golden bugle dangles!

And her jewell'd Garter? Oh, Sin! oh, Shame!
Let Pride and Vanity bear the blame,
That bring such blots on female fame!
  But to be a true recorder,
Besides its thin transparent stuff,
The tunic was loop'd quite high enough
  To give a glimpse of the Order!

But what have sin or shame to do
With a Golden Leg—and a stout one too?
  Away with all Prudery's panics!
That the precious metal, by thick and thin,
Will cover square acres of land or sin,
    Is a fact made plain
    Again and again,
  In Morals as well as Mechanics.

A few, indeed, of her proper sex,
Who seem'd to feel her foot on their necks,
And fear'd their charms would meet with checks
  From so rare and splendid a blazon—
A few cried "fie!"—and "forward!"—and "bold!"
And said of the Leg it might be gold,
  But to them it look'd like brazen!

AND HER PRECIOUS LEG.

'Twas hard they hinted for flesh and blood,
Virtue and Beauty, and all that's good,
 To strike to mere dross their topgallants—
But what were Beauty, or Virtue, or Worth,
Gentle manners, or gentle birth,
Nay what the most talented head on earth
 To a Leg worth fifty Talents!

But the men sang quite another hymn
Of glory and praise to the precious Limb—
Age, sordid Age, admired the whim,
 And its indecorum pardon'd—
While half of the young—ay, more than half—
Bow'd down and worshipp'd the Golden Calf,
 Like the Jews when their hearts were harden'd.

A Golden Leg!—what fancies it fired!
What golden wishes and hopes inspired!
 To give but a mere abridgment—
What a leg to leg-bail Embarrassment's serf!
What a leg for a Leg to take on the turf!
 What a leg for a marching regiment!

A golden Leg!—whatever Love sings,
'Twas worth a bushel of "Plain Gold Rings"
 With which the Romantic wheedles.

MISS KILMANSEGG

'Twas worth all the legs in stockings and socks—
'Twas a leg that might be put in the Stocks,
   N.B.—Not the parish beadle's.

And Lady K. nid-nodded her head,
Lapp'd in a turban fancy-bred,
Just like a love-apple, huge and red,
   Some Mussul-womanish mystery:
     But whatever she meant
       To represent,
   She talk'd like the Muse of History.

She told how the filial leg was lost:
And then how much the gold one cost;
   With its weight to a Trojan fraction:
And how it took off, and how it put on;
And call'd on Devil, Duke, and Don,
Mahomet, Moses, and Prester John,
   To notice its beautiful action.

And then of the Leg she went in quest:
And led it where the light was best;
And made it lay itself up to rest
   In postures for painters' studies:
It cost more tricks and trouble by half,
Than it takes to exhibit a six-legg'd Calf
   To a boothful of country Cuddies.

AND HER PRECIOUS LEG.

Nor yet did the Heiress herself omit
The arts that help to make a hit,
   And preserve a prominent station.
She talk'd and laugh'd far more than her share;
And took a part in " Rich and Rare
Were the gems she wore "—and the gems were there,
   Like a Song with an Illustration.

She even stood up with a Count of France
To dance—alas!—the measures we dance
   When Vanity plays the Piper!

Vanity, Vanity, apt to betray,

And lead all sorts of legs astray,
Wood, or metal, or human clay,—
  Since Satan first play'd the Viper!

But first she doff'd her hunting gear,
And favour'd Tom Tug with her golden spear
  To row with down the river—
A Bonze had her golden bow to hold;
A Hermit her belt and bugle of gold;
  And an Abbot her golden quiver.

And then a space was clear'd on the floor,
And she walk'd the Minuet de la Cour,
With all the pomp of a Pompadour,
  But although she began andante,
Conceive the faces of all the Rout,
When she finished off with a whirligig bout,
And the Precious Leg stuck stiffly out
  Like the leg of a Figuranté!

So the courtly dance was goldenly done,
And golden opinions, of course, it won
  From all different sorts of people—
Chiming, ding-dong, with flattering phrase,
In one vociferous peal of praise,
Like the peal that rings on Royal days
  From Loyalty's parish-steeple.

AND HER PRECIOUS LEG.

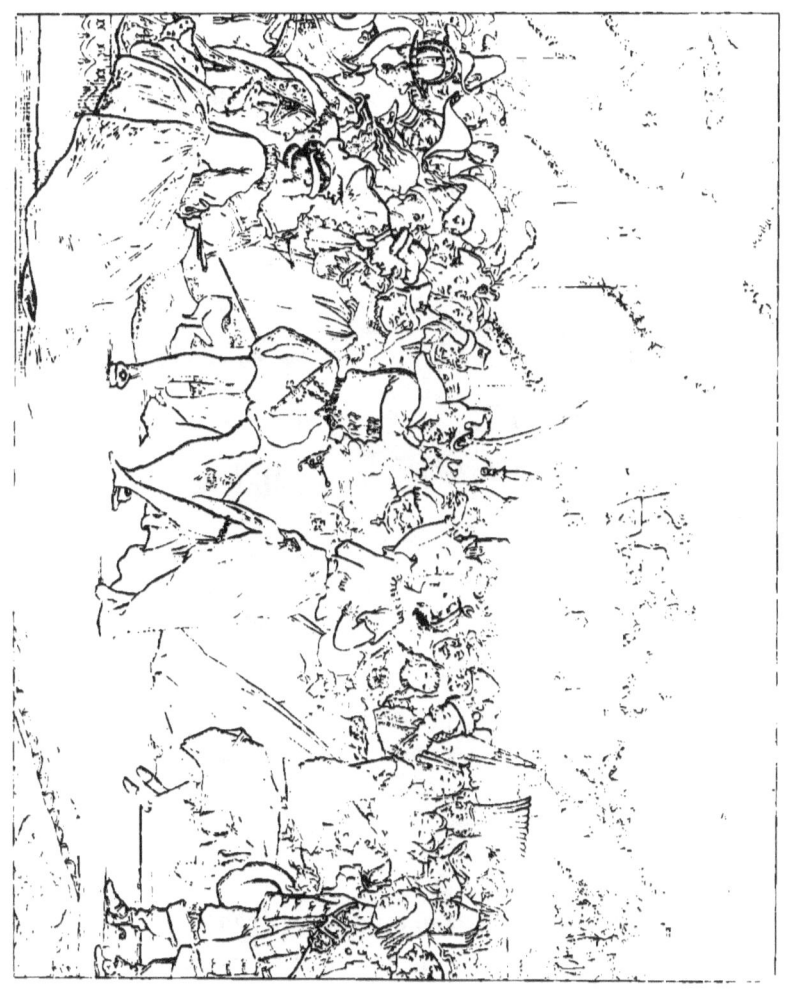

And yet, had the leg been one of those
That dance for bread in flesh-colour'd hose,
  With Rosina's pastoral bevy,
The jeers it had met,—the shouts! the scoff!
The cutting advice to "take itself off,"
  For sounding but half so heavy.

Had it been a leg like those, perchance,
That teach little girls and boys to dance,
To set poussette, recede, and advance,
  With the steps and figures most proper,—
Had it hopp'd for a weekly or quarterly sum,

AND HER PRECIOUS LEG.

How little of praise or grist would have come
   To a mill with such a hopper!

But the Leg was none of those limbs forlorn—
Bartering capers and hops for corn—
That meet with public hisses and scorn,
   Or the morning journal denounces—
Had it pleased to caper from morn till dusk,
There was all the music of "Money Musk"
   In its ponderous bangs and bounces.

But hark;—as slow as the strokes of a pump,
   Lump, thump!
   Thump, lump!
As the Giant of Castle Otranto might stump,
   To a lower room from an upper—
Down she goes with a noisy dint,
For taking the crimson turban's hint,
A noble Lord at the Head of the Mint
   Is leading the Leg to supper!

But the supper, alas! must rest untold,
With its blaze of light and its glitter of gold,
   For to paint that scene of glamour,
It would need the Great Enchanter's charm,
Who waves over Palace, and Cot, and Farm,
An arm like the Goldbeater's Golden Arm
   That wields a Golden Hammer.

He—only He—could fitly state
The Massive Service of Golden Plate,
  With the proper phrase and expansion—
The rare selection of Foreign Wines—
The Alps of Ice and Mountains of Pines,
The punch in Oceans and sugary shrines,
The Temple of Taste from Gunter's Designs—
In short, all that Wealth with a Feast combines,
  In a Splendid Family Mansion.

Suffice it, each mask'd outlandish guest
Ate and drunk of the very best,
  According to critical conners—
And then they pledged the Hostess and Host,
But the Golden Leg was the standing toast,
    And as somebody swore,
    Walk'd off with more
  Than its share of the "Hips!" and honours!

  "Miss KILMANSEGG!—
  Full glasses I beg!—
Miss KILMANSEGG, and her Precious Leg!"
  And away went the bottle careering!
Wine in bumpers! and shouts in peals!
Till the Clown didn't know his head from his heels,
The Mussulman's eyes danced two-some reels,
  And the Quaker was hoarse with cheering!

Her Dream.

Miss KILMANSEGG took off her leg,
And laid it down like a cribbage peg,
  For the Rout was done and the riot:
The Square was hush'd; not a sound was heard;
The sky was gray, and no creature stirr'd,
Except one little precocious bird,
  That chirp'd—and then was quiet.

So still without,—so still within;—
  It had been a sin
  To drop a pin—
So intense is silence after a din,
  It seem'd like Death's rehearsal!
To stir the air no eddy came;
And the taper burnt with as still a flame,
As to flicker had been a burning shame,
  In a calm so universal.

MISS KILMANSEGG

The time for sleep had come at last;
And there was the bed, so soft, so vast,
   Quite a field of Bedfordshire clover;
Softer, cooler, and calmer, no doubt,
From the piece of work just ravell'd out,
For one of the pleasures of having a rout
   Is the pleasure of having it over.

No sordid pallet, or truckle mean,
Of straw, and rug, and tatters unclean;
But a splendid, gilded, carved machine,
   That was fit for a Royal Chamber,
On the top was a gorgeous golden wreath;
And the damask curtains hung beneath,
   Like clouds of crimson and amber;

Curtains, held up by two little plump things,
With golden bodies and golden wings,—
   Mere fins for such solidities—
     Two Cupids, in short,
     Of the regular sort,
   But the housemaid call'd them "Cupidities."

AND HER PRECIOUS LEG.

No patchwork quilt, all seams and scars,
But velvet, powder'd with golden stars,
   A fit mantle for Night-Commanders!
And the pillow, as white as snow undimm'd
And as cool as the pool that the breeze has skimm'd,
Was cased in the finest cambric, and trimm'd
   With the costliest lace of Flanders,

And the bed—of the Eider's softest down,
'Twas a place to revel, to smother, to drown
   In a bliss inferr'd by the Poet;
For if Ignorance be indeed a bliss,
What blessed ignorance equals this,
   To sleep—and not to know it?

Oh, bed! oh, bed! delicious bed!
That heaven upon earth to the weary head;
But a place that to name would be ill-bred,
   To the head with a wakeful trouble—
'Tis held by such a different lease!
To one, a place of comfort and peace,
All stuff'd with the down of stubble geese,
   To another with only the stubble!

MISS KILMANSEGG

To one, a perfect Halcyon nest,
All calm, and balm, and quiet, and rest,
  And soft as the fur of the cony—
To another so restless for body and head,
That the bed seems borrow'd from Nettlebed,
  And the pillow from Stratford the Stony!

To the happy, a first class carriage of ease,
To the Land of Nod or where you please;
  But alas! for the watchers and weepers,
Who turn, and turn, and turn again,
But turn, and turn, and turn in vain,
    With an anxious brain,
    And thoughts in a train
  That does not run upon sleepers!

Wide awake as the mousing owl,
Night-hawk, or other nocturnal fowl,—
  But more profitless vigils keeping,—
Wide awake in the dark they stare,
Filling with phantoms the vacant air,
As if that Crook-back'd Tyrant Care
  Had plotted to kill them sleeping.

AND HER PRECIOUS LEG.

And oh! when the blessed diurnal light
Is quench'd by the providential night,
   To render our slumber more certain,
Pity, pity the wretches that weep,

For they must be wretched who cannot sleep
   When God himself draws the curtain!

The careful Betty the pillow beats,
And airs the blankets, and smooths the sheets,
   And gives the mattress a shaking—

But vainly Betty performs her part,
If a ruffled head and a rumpled heart
   As well as the couch want making.

There's Morbid, all bile, and verjuice, and nerves,
Where other people would make preserves,
   He turns his fruits into pickles:
Jealous, envious, and fretful by day,
At night, to his own sharp fancies a prey,
He lies like a hedgehog roll'd up the wrong way,
   Tormenting himself with his prickles.

But a child—that bids the world good-night,
In downright earnest and cuts it quite—
   A Cherub no Art can copy,—
'Tis a perfect picture to see him lie
As if he had supp'd on a dormouse pie,
(An ancient classical dish by-the-bye)
   With a sauce of syrup of poppy.

Oh, bed! bed! bed! delicious bed!
That heaven upon earth to the weary head,
   Whether lofty or low its condition!
But instead of putting our plagues on shelves,
In our blankets how often we toss ourselves,
Or are toss'd by such allegorical elves
   As Pride, Hate, Greed, and Ambition!

AND HER PRECIOUS LEG.

The independent Miss KILMANSEGG
Took off her independent Leg
  And laid it beneath her pillow,
And then on the bed her frame she cast,
The time for repose had come at last,
But long, long after the storm is past
  Rolls the turbid, turbulent billow.

No part she had in vulgar cares
That belong to common household affairs—
Nocturnal annoyances such as theirs

MISS KILMANSEGG

Who lie with a shrewd surmising
That while they are couchant (a bitter cup!)
Their bread and butter are getting up,
   And the coals—confound them! are rising.

No fear she had her sleep to postpone,
Like the crippled Widow that weeps alone,
And cannot make a doze her own,
   For the dread that may hap on the morrow,
The true and Christian reading to baulk,
A broker will take up her bed and walk,
   By way of curing her sorrow.

No cause like these she had to bewail:
But the breath of applause had blown a gale,
And winds from that quarter seldom fail
   To cause some human commotion;
But whenever such breezes coincide
     With the very spring-tide
     Of human pride,
There's no such swell on the ocean!

AND HER PRECIOUS LEG.

Peace, and ease, and slumber lost,
She turn'd, and roll'd, and tumbled, and toss'd,
   With a tumult that would not settle:
A common case, indeed, with such
As have too little, or think too much,
   Of the precious and glittering metal.

Gold!—she saw at her golden foot
The Peer whose tree had an olden root,
The Proud, the Great, the Learned to boot,
   The handsome, the gay, and the witty—
The Man of Science—of Arms—of Art,
The man who deals but at Pleasure's mart,
   And the man who deals in the City.

Gold, still Gold—and true to the mould!
In the very scheme of her dream it told;
  For, by magical transmutation,
From her Leg through her body it seem'd to go,
Till, gold above, and gold below,
She was gold, all gold, from her little gold toe
  To her organ of Veneration!

And still she retain'd through Fancy's art,
The Golden Bow, and Golden Dart,
With which she had play'd a Goddess's part
  In her recent glorification.
And still like one of the self-same brood,
On a Plinth of the self-same metal she stood
  For the whole world's adoration.

And hymns of incense around her roll'd,
From Golden Harps and Censers of Gold,—
For Fancy in dreams is as uncontroll'd
  As a horse without a bridle:
What wonder, then, from all checks exempt,
If, inspired by the Golden Leg, she dreamt
  She was turn'd to a Golden Idol?

AND HER PRECIOUS LEG.

Her Courtship.

When leaving Eden's happy land
The grieving Angel led by the hand
　Our banish'd Father and Mother,
Forgotten amid their awful doom,
The tears, the fears, and the future's gloom,
On each brow was a wreath of Paradise bloom,
　That our Parents had twined for each other.

It was only while sitting like figures of stone,
For the grieving Angel had skyward flown,
As they sat, those Two in the world alone,
　With disconsolate hearts nigh cloven,
That scenting the gust of happier hours,
They look'd around for the precious flow'rs,
And lo!—a last relic of Eden's dear bow'rs—
　The chaplets that Love had woven!

AND HER PRECIOUS LEG.

MISS KILMANSEGG

And still, when a pair of Lovers meet,
There's a sweetness in air, unearthly sweet,
That savours still of that happy retreat
   Where Eve by Adam was courted:
Whilst the joyous Thrush, and the gentle Dove,
Woo'd their mates in the boughs above,
   And the Serpent, as yet, only sported.

Who hath not felt that breath in the air,
A perfume and freshness strange and rare,
A warmth in the light, and a bliss everywhere,
   When young hearts yearn together?
All sweets below, and all sunny above,
Oh! there's nothing in life like making love,
   Save making hay in fine weather!

Who hath not found amongst his flow'rs
A blossom too bright for this world of ours,
   Like a rose among snows of Sweden?
But to turn again to Miss KILMANSEGG,
Where must Love have gone to beg,
If such a thing as a Golden Leg
   Had put its foot in Eden!

AND HER PRECIOUS LEG.

And yet—to tell the rigid truth—
Her favour was sought by Age and Youth—
　For the prey will find a prowler!
She was follow'd, flatter'd, courted, address'd,
Woo'd, and coo'd, and wheedled, and press'd,
By suitors from North, South, East, and West,
　Like that Heiress in song, Tibbie Fowler!

But, alas! alas! for the Woman's fate,
Who has from a mob to choose a mate!
　'Tis a strange and painful mystery!
But the more the eggs, the worse the hatch;
The more the fish, the worse the catch;
The more the sparks, the worse the match;
　Is a fact in Woman's history.

Give her between a brace to pick,
And, mayhap, with luck to help the trick,
She will take the Faustus, and leave the Old Nick—
　But her future bliss to baffle,
Amongst a score let her have a voice,
And she'll have as little cause to rejoice,
As if she had won the "Man of her choice"
　In a matrimonial raffle!

MISS KILMANSEGG

Thus, even thus, with the Heiress and Hope,
Fulfilling the adage of too much rope,
  With so ample a competition,
She chose the least worthy of all the group,
Just as the vulture makes a stoop,
And singles out from the herd or troop
  The beast of the worst condition.

A Foreign Count—who came incog.,
Not under a cloud, but under a fog,

In a Calais packet's fore cabin,

AND HER PRECIOUS LEG.

To charm some lady British-born,
With his eyes as black as the fruit of the thorn,
And his hooky nose, and beard half-shorn,
Like a half-converted Rabbin.

And because the Sex confess a charm
In the man who has slash'd a head or arm,
Or has been a throat's undoing,
He was dress'd like one of the glorious trade,
At least when glory is off parade,
With a stock, and a frock, well trimm'd with braid,
And frogs—that went a-wooing.

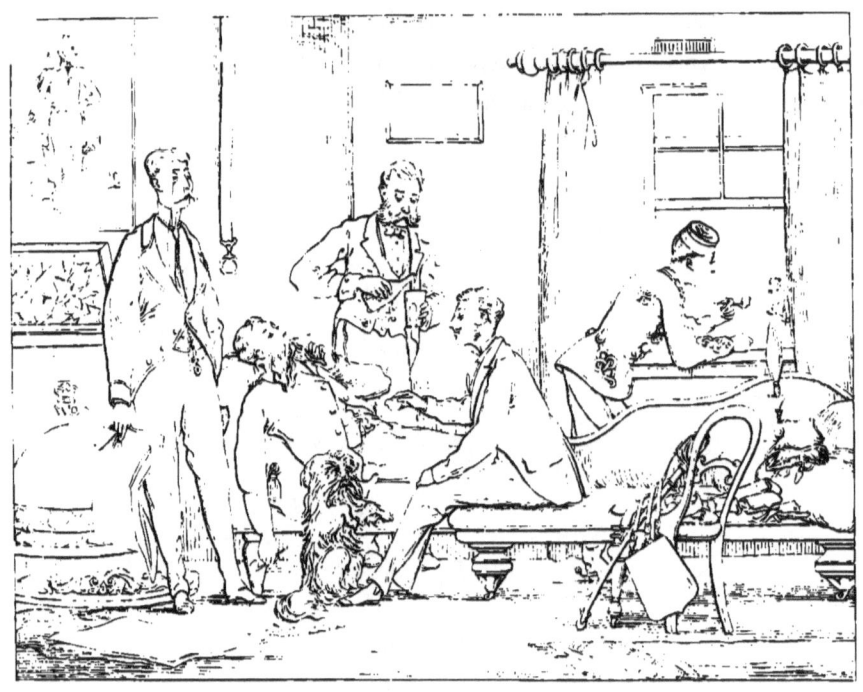

Moreover, as counts are apt to do,
On the left hand side of his dark surtout,
At one of those holes that buttons go through,
  (To be a precise recorder,)
A ribbon he wore, or rather a scrap,
About an inch of ribbon mayhap,
That one of his rivals, a whimsical chap,
  Described as his "Retail Order."

AND HER PRECIOUS LEG.

And then—and much it help'd his chance—
He could sing, and play first fiddle, and dance,
Perform charades, and Proverbs of France—
  Act the tender, and do the cruel;
For amongst his other killing parts,
He had broken a brace of female hearts,

And murder'd three men in duel!

Savage at heart, and false of tongue,
Subtle with age, and smooth to the young,
  Like a snake in his coiling and curling—
Such was the Count—to give him a niche—

MISS KILMANSEGG

Who came to court that Heiress rich,
And knelt at her foot—one needn't say which—
  Besieging her castle of STERLING.

With pray'rs and vows he open'd his trench,
And plied her with English, Spanish, and French,
  In phrases the most sentimental:
And quoted poems in High and Low Dutch,
With now and then an Italian touch,
Till she yielded, without resisting much,
  To homage so continental.

And then—the sordid bargain to close—
With a miniature sketch of his hooky nose,
And his dear dark eyes, as black as sloes,
And his beard and whiskers, as black as those,
  The lady's consent he requited—
And instead of the lock that lovers beg,
The count received from Miss KILMANSEGG
A model, in small, of her Precious leg—
  And so the couple were plighted!

But, oh! the love that gold must crown!
Better—better, the love of the clown,
Who admires his lass in her Sunday gown,
  As if all the fairies had dress'd her!

AND HER PRECIOUS LEG.

Whose brain to no crooked thought gives birth,
Except that he never will part on earth
  With his true love's crooked tester!

Alas! for the love that's link'd with gold!
Better—better a thousand times told—
  More honest, happy, and laudable,

The downright loving of pretty Cis,
Who wipes her lips though there's nothing amiss,

And takes a kiss, and gives a kiss,
  In which her heart is audible!

Pretty Cis, so smiling and bright,
Who loves—as she labours—with all her might,
  And without any sordid leaven!
Who blushes as red as haws and hips,
Down to her very finger-tips,
For Roger's blue ribbons—to her, like strips
  Cut out of the azure of Heaven!

Her Marriage.

'Twas morn—a most auspicious one!
From the Golden East, the Golden Sun
Came forth his glorious race to run,
  Through clouds of most splendid tinges;
Clouds that lately slept in shade,
    But now seem'd made
    Of gold brocade,
  With magnificent golden fringes.

Gold above, and gold below,
The earth reflected the golden glow,

AND HER PRECIOUS LEG.

From river, and hill, and valley;
Gilt by the golden light of morn,
The Thames—it look'd like the Golden Horn,
And the Barge, that carried coal or corn,
　Like Cleopatra's Galley!

Bright as clusters of Golden-rod,
Suburban poplars began to nod,
　With extempore splendour furnish'd;
While London was bright with glittering clocks,
Golden dragons, and Golden cocks,
　　And above them all,
　　The dome of St. Paul,
With its Golden Cross and its Golden Ball,
　Shone out as if newly burnish'd!

And lo! for Golden Hours and Joys,
Troops of glittering Golden Boys
Danced along with a jocund noise,
　And their gilded emblems carried!
In short, 'twas the year's most Golden Day,
By mortals call'd the First of May,
　　When Miss KILMANSEGG,
　　Of the Golden Leg,
　With a Golden Ring was married!

MISS KILMANSEGG

And thousands of children, women, and men,
Counted the clock from eight till ten
　From St. James's sonorous steeple;
For next to that interesting job,
The hanging of Jack, or Bill, or Bob,
There's nothing so draws a London mob
　As the noosing of very rich people.

And a treat it was for the mob to behold

The Bridal Carriage that blazed with gold!
And the Footmen tall, and the Coachman bold,
　In liveries so resplendent—
Coats you wonder'd to see in place
They seem'd so rich with golden lace,
　That they might have been independent.

AND HER PRECIOUS LEG.

Coats that made those menials proud
Gaze with scorn on the dingy crowd,
   From their gilded elevations;
Not to forget that saucy lad
(Ostentation's favourite cad),
The Page, who look'd, so splendidly clad,
   Like a Page of the "Wealth of Nations."

But the Coachman carried off the state,
With what was a Lancashire body of late
   Turn'd into a Dresden Figure;
With a bridal Nosegay of early bloom,
About the size of a birchen broom,
And so huge a White Favour, had Gog been Groom
   He need not have worn a bigger.

And then to see the Groom! the Count!
With Foreign Orders to such an amount,
   And whiskers so wild—nay, bestial;
He seem'd to have borrow'd the shaggy hair
As well as the stars of the Polar Bear,
   To make him look celestial!

And then—Great Jove!—the struggle, the crush,
The screams, the heaving, the awful rush,
   The swearing, the tearing, and fighting,—

MISS KILMANSEGG

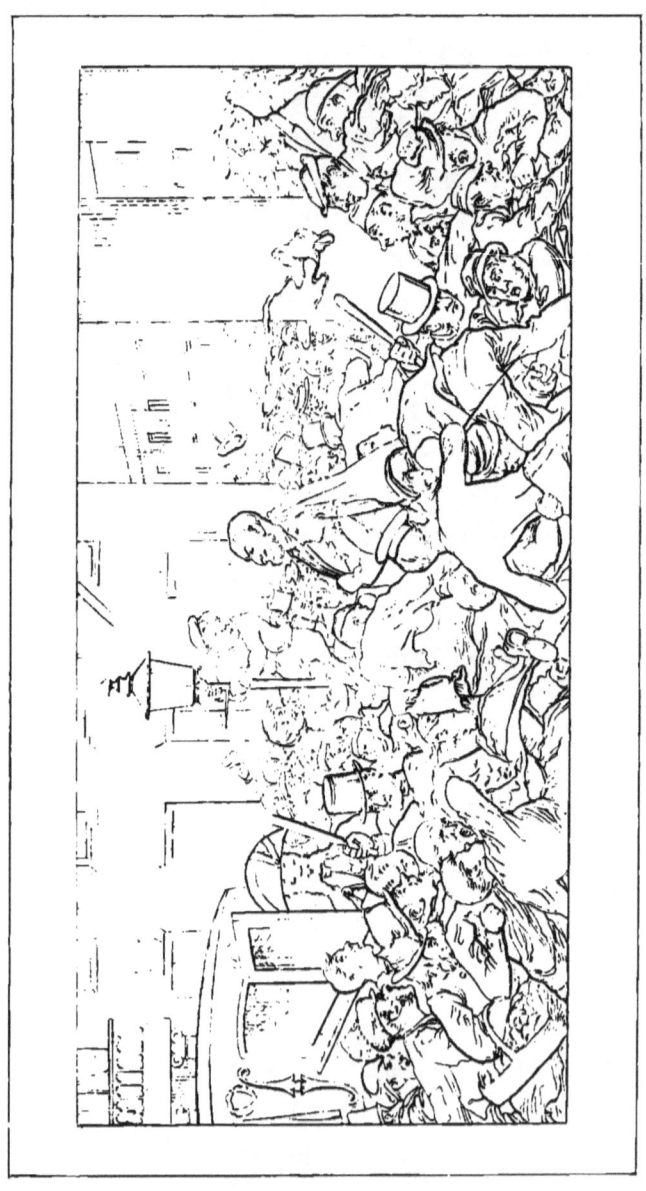

AND HER PRECIOUS LEG.

The hats and bonnets smash'd like an egg—
To catch a glimpse of the Golden Leg,
Which, between the steps and Miss KILMANSEGG,
 Was fully display'd in alighting!

From the Golden Ankle to the Knee
There it was for the mob to see!
A shocking act had it chanced to be
 A crooked leg or a skinny:
But although a magnificent veil she wore,
Such as never was seen before,
In case of blushes, she blush'd no more
 Than GEORGE the FIRST on a guinea!

Another step, and lo! she was launch'd!
All in white, as Brides are blanch'd,
 With a wreath of most wonderful splendour—
Diamonds, and pearls, so rich in device,
That, according to calculation nice,
Her head was worth as royal a price
 As the head of the Young Pretender.

MISS KILMANSEGG

Bravely she shone—and shone the more
As she sail'd through the crowd of squalid and poor
   Thief, beggar, and tatterdemalion—
Led by the Count, with his sloe-black eyes
Bright with triumph and some surprise,
Like Anson on making sure of his prize
   The famous Mexican Galleon.

Anon came Lady K. with her face
Quite made up to act with grace,
   But she cut the performance shorter;
For instead of pacing stately and stiff,
At the stare of the vulgar she took a miff,
And ran, full speed, into Church as if
   To get married before her daughter.

But Sir Jacob walk'd more slowly, and bow'd
Right and left to the gaping crowd,
   Wherever a glance was seizable;
For Sir Jacob thought he bow'd like a GUELPH,
And therefore bow'd to imp and elf,
And would gladly have made a bow to himself,
   Had such a bow been feasible.

AND HER PRECIOUS LEG.

And last—and not the least of the sight,
Six " Handsome Fortune's," all in white,
Came to help in the marriage rite,—
    And rehearse their own hymeneals;

And then the bright procession to close,
They were followed by just as many Beaux
   Quite fine enough for Ideals.

Glittering men, and splendid dames,
Thus they enter'd the porch of St. James',
   Pursued by a thunder of laughter;
For the Beadle was forced to intervene,
For Jim the Crow, and his Mayday Queen,
With her gilded ladle, and Jack i' the Green,
   Would fain have follow'd after!

Beadle-like he hush'd the shout;
But the temple was full "inside and out,"
And a buzz kept buzzing all round about
   Like bees when the day is sunny—
A buzz universal that interfered
With the rite that ought to have been revered,
As if the couple already were smear'd
   With Wedlock's treacle and honey!

Yet Wedlock's a very awful thing!
'Tis something like that feat in the ring
   Which requires good nerve to do it—

AND HER PRECIOUS LEG.

When one of a "Grand Equestrian Troop"
Makes a jump at a gilded hoop,
   Not certain at all
   Of what may befall
After his getting through it!

But the Count he felt the nervous work
No more than any polygamous Turk,

Or bold piratical skipper,
Who, during his buccaneering search,
Would as soon engage "a hand" in church
As a hand on board his clipper!

And how did the Bride perform her part?
Like any Bride who is cold at heart,
  Mere snow with the ice's glitter;
What but a life of winter for her!
Bright but chilly, alive without stir,

AND HER PRECIOUS LEG.

So splendidly comfortless,—just like a Fir
When the frost is severe and bitter.

Such were the future man and wife!
Whose bale or bliss to the end of life
　A few short words were to settle—
　　"Wilt thou have this woman?"
　　　"I will"—and then,
　　"Wilt thou have this man?"
　　　"I will," and "Amen"—
And those Two were one Flesh, in the Angels' ken,
　Except one Leg—that was metal.

Then the names were sign'd—and kiss'd the kiss:
And the Bride, who came from her coach a Miss,
　As a Countess walk'd to her carriage—
Whilst Hymen preen'd his plumes like a dove,
And Cupid flutter'd his wings above,
In the shape of a fly—as little a Love
　As ever look'd in at a marriage!

Another crash—and away they dash'd,
And the gilded carriage and footmen flash'd
　From the eyes of the gaping people—

Who turn'd to gaze at the toe-and-heel
Of the Golden Boys beginning a reel,
To the merry sound of a wedding peal
   From St. James' musical steeple.

Those wedding-bells! those wedding-bells!
How sweetly they sound in pastoral dells
   From a tow'r in an ivy-green jacket!
But town-made joys how dearly they cost;
And after all are tumbled and tost,
Like a peal from a London steeple, and lost
   In town-made riot and racket.

The wedding-peal, how sweetly it peals
With grass or heather beneath our heels,—
   For bells are Music's laughter!—
But a London peal, well mingled, be sure,
With vulgar noises and voices impure,
What a harsh and discordant overture
   To the Harmony meant to come after!

But hence with Discord—perchance, too soon
To cloud the face of the honeymoon
   With a dismal occultation!—

AND HER PRECIOUS LEG.

Whatever Fate's concerted trick,
The Countess and Count, at the present nick,
Have a chicken and not a crow to pick
    At a sumptuous Cold Collation.

A Breakfast—no unsubstantial mess,
But one in the style of Good Queen Bess,
    Who,—hearty as hippocampus,—
Broke her fast with ale and beef,
Instead of toast and the Chinese leaf,
    And—in lieu of anchovy—grampus!

A breakfast of fowl, and fish, and flesh,
Whatever was sweet, or salt, or fresh;
    With wines the most rare and curious—
Wines, of the richest flavour and hue;
With fruits from the worlds both Old and New;
And fruits obtain'd before they were due
    At a discount most usurious.

For wealthy palates there be, that scout
What is in season, for what is out,
    And prefer all precocious savour:
For instance, early green peas, of the sort
That costs some four or five guineas a quart;
    Where the Mint is the principal flavour.

MISS KILMANSEGG

And many a wealthy man was there,
Such as the wealthy City could spare,
  To put in a portly appearance—
Men, whom their fathers had help'd to gild:
And men, who had had their fortunes to build
And—much to their credit—had richly fill'd
  Their purses by pursy-verance.

Men, by popular rumour at least,
Not the last to enjoy a feast!
  And truly they were not idle!
Luckier far than the chesnut tits,
Which, down at the door, stood champing their bits,
  At a different sort of bridle.

For the time was come—and the whisker'd Count
Help'd his Bride in the carriage to mount,
  And fain would the Muse deny it,
But the crowd, including two butchers in blue,
(The regular killing Whitechapel hue,)
Of her Precious Calf had as ample a view,
  As if they had come to buy it!

Then away! away! with all the speed
That golden spurs can give to the steed,—

AND HER PRECIOUS LEG.

Both Yellow Boys and Guineas, indeed,
    Concurr'd to urge the cattle—
Away they went, with favours white,
Yellow jackets and panels bright,
And left the mob, like a mob at night,
    Agape at the sound of a rattle.

Away, away, they rattled and roll'd,
The COUNT, and his BRIDE, and her LEG of GOLD—
    That faded charm to the charmer,
Away through Old Brentford rang the din,
Of wheels and heels, on their way to win
That hill, named after one of her kin,
    The Hill of the Golden Farmer!

Gold, still gold—it flew like dust!
It tipp'd the post-boy, and paid the trust;
In each open palm it was freely thrust;
    There was nothing but giving and taking!
And if gold could insure the future hour,
What hopes attended that BRIDE to her bow'r,
But alas! even hearts with a four-horse pow'r
    Of opulence end in breaking!

Her Honeymoon.

    The moon—the moon, so silver and cold,
    Her fickle temper has oft been told,
      Now shady—now bright and sunny—
    But of all the lunar things that change,
    The one that shows most fickle and strange,

AND HER PRECIOUS LEG.

And takes the most eccentric range
Is the moon—so call'd—of honey!

To some a full grown orb reveal'd,
As big and as round as Norval's shield,
   And as bright as a burner Bude-lighted;
To others as dud, and dingy, and damp,
As any oleaginous lamp,
Of the regular old parochial stamp,
   In a London fog benighted.

To the loving, a bright and constant sphere,
That makes earth's commonest scenes appear
   All poetic, romantic, and tender:
Hanging with jewels a cabbage-stump,
And investing a common post, or a pump,
A currant-bush, or a gooseberry clump,
   With a halo of dreamlike splendour.

A sphere such as shone from Italian skies,
In Juliet's dear, dark, liquid eyes,
   Tipping trees with its ardent braveries—
And to couples not favour'd with Fortune's boons
One of the most delightful of moons.

MISS KILMANSEGG

AND HER PRECIOUS LEG.

For it brightens their pewter platters and spoons
   Like a silver service of SAVORY'S!

For all is bright, and beauteous, and clear,
And the meanest thing most precious and dear,
   When the magic of love is present:
Love, that lends a sweetness and grace
To the humblest spot and the plainest face—
That turns Wilderness Row into Paradise Place,
   And Garlick Hill to Mount Pleasant!

Love that sweetens sugarless tea,
And makes contentment and joy agree
   With the coarsest boarding and bedding:
Love that no golden ties can attach,
But nestles under the humblest thatch,
And will fly away from an Emperor's match
   To dance at a Penny Wedding!

Oh, happy, happy, thrice happy state,
When such a bright Planet governs the fate
   Of a pair of united lovers!
'Tis theirs, in spite of the Serpent's hiss,
To enjoy the pure primeval kiss,

With as much of the old original bliss
As mortality ever recovers!

There's strength in double joints, no doubt,
In double X Ale, and Dublin Stout,
That the single sorts know nothing about—
   And the fist is strongest when doubled—
And double aqua-fortis, of course,
And double soda-water, perforce,
   Are the strongest that ever bubbled!

There's double beauty whenever a Swan
Swims on a Lake, with her double thereon;
And ask the gardener, Luke or John,
   Of the beauty of double-blowing—
A double dahlia delights the eye;
And its far the loveliest sight in the sky
   When a double rainbow is glowing!

There's warmth in a pair of double soles;
As well as a double allowance of coals—
   In a coat that is double-breasted—
In double windows and double doors;
And a double U wind is blest by scores
   For its warmth to the tender-chested.

AND HER PRECIOUS LEG.

There's a twofold sweetness in double pipes;
And a double barrel and double snipes
    Give the sportsman a duplicate pleasure:
There's double safety in double locks;
And double letters bring cash for the box;
And all the world knows that double knocks
    Are gentility's double measure.

There's a double sweetness in double rhymes,
And a double at Whist and a double Times
    In profit are certainly double—

MISS KILMANSEGG

By doubling, the Hare contrives to escape:
And all seamen delight in a doubled Cape,
And a double reef'd topsail in trouble.

There's a double chuck at a double chin,
And of course there's a double pleasure therein,
   If the parties were brought to telling:
And however our Dennises take offence,
A double meaning shows double sense;
     And if proverbs tell truth,
     A double tooth
   Is Wisdom's adopted dwelling!

But double wisdom, and pleasure, and sense,
Beauty, respect, strength, comfort, and thence
   Through whatever the list discovers,
They are all in the double blessedness summ'd,
Of what was formerly double drumm'd,
   The Marriage of two true Lovers!

Now the KILMANSEGG Moon, it must be told—
Though instead of silver it tipp'd with gold—
Shone rather wan, and distant, and cold,
   And before its days were at thirty,
Such gloomy clouds began to collect,
With an ominous ring of ill effect,
As gave but too much cause to expect
   Such weather as seamen call dirty!

AND HER PRECIOUS LEG.

And yet the moon was the "Young May Moon,"
And the scented hawthorn had blossom'd soon,
   And the thrush and the blackbird were singing—
The snow-white lambs were skipping in play,
And the bee was humming a tune all day
To flowers, as welcome as flowers in May,
   And the trout in the stream was springing!

But what were the hues of the blooming earth
Its scents—its sounds—or the music and mirth
   Of its furr'd or its feather'd creatures,
To a Pair in the world's last sordid stage,
Who had never look'd into nature's page,
And had strange ideas of a Golden Age,
   Without any Arcadian features?

And what were joys of the pastoral kind
To a Bride—town made—with a heart and a mind
   With simplicity ever at battle?
A bride of an ostentatious race,
Who, thrown in the Golden Farmer's place,
Would have trimm'd her shepherds with golden lace,
   And gilt the horns of her cattle.

She could not please the pigs with her whim,
And the sheep wouldn't cast their eyes at a limb
   For which she had been such a martyr:
The deer in the park, and the colts at grass,

And the cows unheeded let it pass:
And the ass on the common was such an ass,
   That he wouldn't have swapp'd
   The thistle he cropp'd
  For her Leg, including the Garter!

She hated lanes and she hated fields—
She hated all that the country yields—
   And barely knew turnips from clover;
She hated walking in any shape,
And a country stile was an awkward scrape,
Without the bribe of a mob to gape
  At the Leg in clambering over!

O blessed nature. "Orus! Orus!"
Who cannot sigh for the country thus,
   Absorb'd in a worldly torpor—
Who does not yearn for its meadow sweet breath,
Untainted by care, and crime, and death,
And to stand sometimes upon grass or heath—
  That soul, spite of gold, is a pauper!

But to hail the pearly advent of morn,
And relish the odour fresh from the thorn,
   She was far too pamper'd a madam—
Or to joy in the daylight waxing strong,
While, after ages of sorrow and wrong
The scorn of the proud, the misrule of the strong,

AND HER PRECIOUS LEG.

And all the woes that to man belong,
The Lark still carols the self-same song
   That he did to the uncurst Adam!

The Lark! she had given all Leipsic's flocks
For a Vauxhall tune in a musical box;
   And as for the birds in the thicket,
Thrush or ousel in leafy niche,
The linnet or finch she was far too rich

To care for a Morning Concert to which
   She was welcome without any ticket.

Gold, still gold, her standard of old,
All pastoral joys were tried by gold,
　Or by fancies golden and crural—
Till ere she had pass'd one week unblest,
As her agricultural Uncle's guest,
Her mind was made up, and fully imprest,
　That felicity could not be rural!

And the Count?—to the snow-white lambs at play,
And all the scents and the sights of May,
　And the birds that warbled their passion,
His ears, and dark eyes, and decided nose,
Were as deaf and as blind and as dull as those
That overlook the Bouquet de Rose,
　　The Huile Antique,
　　And Parfum Unique,
　In a Barber's Temple of Fashion.

To tell, indeed, the true extent
Of his rural bias, so far it went
　As to covet estates in ring fences—
And for rural lore he had learn'd in town
That the country was green, turn'd up with brown,
And garnish'd with trees that a man might cut down
　Instead of his own expenses.

AND HER PRECIOUS LEG.

And yet had that fault been his only one,
The Pair might have had few quarrels or none,
  For their tastes thus far were in common;
But faults he had that a haughty bride
With a Golden Leg could hardly abide—
Faults that would even have roused the pride
  Of a far less metalsome woman!

It was early days indeed for a wife,
In the very spring of her married life,
  To be chill'd by its wintry weather—
But instead of sitting as Love-Birds do,
Or Hymen's turtles that bill and coo—
Enjoying their "moon and honey for two"
  They were scarcely seen together!

In vain she sat with her Precious Leg
A little exposed, à la KILMANSEGG,
  And roll'd her eyes in their sockets!
He left her in spite of her tender regards,
And those loving murmurs described by bards,
For the rattling of dice and the shuffling of cards,
  And the poking of balls into pockets

MISS KILMANSEGG

Moreover he loved the deepest stake
And the heaviest bets the players would make;
   And he drank—the reverse of sparely,—
And he used strange curses that made her fret;
And when he play'd with herself at piquet,
     She found, to her cost,
      For she always lost,
   That the Count did not count quite fairly.

And then came dark mistrust and doubt,
Gather'd by worming his secrets out,
   And slips in his conversations—
Fears, which all her peace destroy'd,
That his title was null—his coffers were void—
And his French Chateau was in Spain, or enjoy'd
   The most airy of situations.

But still his heart—if he had such a part—
She—only she—might possess his heart,
   And hold his affections in fetters—
Alas! that hope, like a crazy ship,
Was forced its anchor and cable to slip
When, seduced by her fears, she took a dip
   In his private papers and letters.

AND HER PRECIOUS LEG.

Letters that told of dangerous leagues;
And notes that hinted as many intrigues
   As the Count's in the "Barber of Seville"—
In short such mysteries came to light,
That the Countess-Bride, on the thirtieth night,
Woke and started up in affright,
And kick'd and scream'd with all her might,
And finally fainted away outright,
   For she dreamt she had married the Devil!

Her Misery.

Who hath not met with home-made bread,
A heavy compound of putty and lead—
And home-made wines that rack the head,
   And home-made liqueurs and waters?
Home-made pop that will not foam,
And home-made dishes that drive one from home,
     Not to name each mess,
     For the face or dress,
   Home-made by the homely daughters?

Home-made physic that sickens the sick;
Thick for thin and thin for thick;—
In short, each homogeneous trick
   For poisoning domesticity?
And since our Parents, call'd the First,
A little family squabble nurst,
Of all our evils the worst of the worst
   Is home-made infelicity.

There's a Golden Bird that claps its wings,
And dances for joy on its perch, and sings

AND HER PRECIOUS LEG.

With a Persian exultation:
For the Sun is shining into the room,
And brightens up the carpet-bloom,
As if it were new, bran new, from the loom,
    Or the lone Nun's fabrication.

And thence the glorious radiance flames
On pictures in massy gilded frames—
Enshrining, however, no painted Dames,
    But portraits of colts and fillies—
Pictures hanging on walls, which shine,
In spite of the bard's familiar line,
    With clusters of "Gilded lilies."

And still the flooding sunlight shares
Its lustre with gilded sofas and chairs,
    That shine as if freshly burnish'd—
And gilded tables, with glittering stocks
Of gilded china, and golden clocks,
Toy, and trinket, and musical box,
    That Peace and Paris have furnish'd.

And lo! with the brightest gleam of all
The glowing sunbeam is seen to fall
    On an object as rare as splendid—

MISS KILMANSEGG

The golden foot of the Golden Leg
Of the Countess—once Miss KILMANSEGG—
But there all sunshine is ended.

Her cheek is pale, and her eye is dim,
And downward cast, yet not at the limb,
   Once the centre of all speculation;
But downward drooping in comfort's dearth,
As gloomy thoughts are drawn to the earth—
Whence human sorrows derive their birth—
   By a moral gravitation.

Her golden hair is out of its braids,
And her sighs betray the gloomy shades
   That her evil planet revolves in—
And tears are falling that catch a gleam
So bright as they drop in the sunny beam,
That tears of aqua regia they seem,
   The water that gold dissolves in!

Yet not in filial grief were shed
   Those tears for a mother's insanity;
Nor yet because her father was dead,

AND HER PRECIOUS LEG.

For the bowing Sir Jacob had bow'd his head
　To Death—with his usual urbanity;
The waters that down her visage rill'd
Were drops of unrectified spirit distill'd
　From the limbeck of Pride and Vanity.

Tears that fell alone and uncheckt,
Without relief, and without respect,
Like the fabled pearls that pigs neglect,
　When pigs have that opportunity—
And of all the griefs that mortals share,

MISS KILMANSEGG

The one that seems the hardest to bear
Is the grief without community.

How bless'd the heart that has a friend
A sympathising ear to lend
To troubles too great to smother!
For as ale and porter, when flat, are restored
Till a sparkling bubbling head they afford,

So sorrow is cheer'd by being pour'd
From one vessel into another.

AND HER PRECIOUS LEG.

But friend or gossip she had not one
To hear the vile deeds that the Count had done,
   How night after night he rambled;
And how she had learn'd by sad degrees
That he drank, and smoked, and worse than these,
   That he "swindled, intrigued, and gambled."

How he kiss'd the maids, and sparr'd with John;
And came to bed with his garments on;
   With other offences as heinous—
And brought strange gentlemen home to dine,
That he said were in the Fancy Line,
And they fancied spirits instead of wine,
   And call'd her lap-dog "Venus."

Of "making a book" how he made a stir,
But never had written a line to her,
   Once his idol and Cara Sposa:
And how he had storm'd, and treated her ill,
Because she refused to go down to a mill,
She didn't know where but remember'd still
   That the Miller's name was MENDOZA.

How often he waked her up at night,
And oftener still by the morning light,
   Reeling home from his haunts unlawful;
Singing songs that shouldn't be sung,

Except by beggars and thieves unhung—
Or volleying oaths, that a foreign tongue
  Made still more horrid and awful!

How oft, instead of otto of rose,
With vulgar smells he offended her nose,
  From gin, tobacco, and onion!
And then how wildly he used to stare!

And shake his fist at nothing, and swear,—

AND HER PRECIOUS LEG.

And pluck by the handful his shaggy hair,
Till he look'd like a study of Giant Despair
For a new Edition of BUNYAN!

For dice will run the contrary way,
As well is known to all who play,
  And cards will conspire as in treason:
And what with keeping a hunting box,
      Following fox—
      Friends in flocks,
      Burgundies, Hocks,
      From London Docks;
      Stultz's frocks,
      Manton and Nock's
      Barrels and locks,
      Shooting blue rocks,
      Trainers and jocks,
      Buskins and socks,
      Pugilistical knocks,
      And fighting-cocks,
If he found himself short in funds and stocks,
  These rhymes will furnish the reason!

His friends, indeed, were falling away—
Friends who insist on play or pay—

MISS KILMANSEGG

And he fear'd at no very distant day
    To be cut by Lord and by cadger,
As one who was gone or going to smash,
For his checks no longer drew the cash,
Because, as his comrades explain'd in flash,
    "He had overdrawn his badger."

Gold, gold—alas! for the gold
Spent where souls are bought and sold,
    In Vice's Walpurgis revel!
Alas! for muffles, and bull-dogs, and guns,
The leg that walks, and the leg that runs,
All real evils, though Fancy ones,
When they lead to debt, dishonour, and duns,
    Nay, to death, and perchance the devil!

Alas! for the last of a Golden race!
Had she cried her wrongs in the market-place,
    She had warrant for all her clamour—
For the worst of rogues, and brutes, and rakes,
Was breaking her heart by constant aches,
With as little remorse as the Pauper who breaks
    A flint with a parish hammer!

AND HER PRECIOUS LEG.

Her Last Will.

Now the Precious Leg while cash was flush,
Or the Count's acceptance worth a rush,
   Had never excited dissension;
But no sooner the stocks began to fall,
Than, without any ossification at all,
The limb became what people call
   A perfect bone of contention.

For alter'd days brought alter'd ways,
And instead of the complimentary phrase,
   So current before her bridal—
The Countess heard, in language low,
That her Precious Leg was precious slow,
A good 'un to look at but bad to go,
   And kept quite a sum lying idle.

That instead of playing musical airs,
Like COLIN's foot in going up stairs—
As the wife in the Scottish ballad declares—
   It made an infernal stumping.
Whereas a member of cork, or wood,
Would be lighter and cheaper and quite as good,
   Without the unbearable thumping.

P'rhaps she thought it a decent thing,
To show her calf to cobbler and king,
 But nothing could be absurder—
While none but the crazy would advertise
Their gold before their servants' eyes,
Who of course some night would make it a prize,
 By a Shocking and Barbarous Murder.

But spite of hint, and threat, and scoff,
 The Leg kept its situation:
For legs are not to be taken off
 By a verbal amputation.
And mortals when they take a whim,
The greater the folly the stiffer the limb
 That stand upon it or by it—
So the Countess, then Miss KILMANSEGG,
At her marriage refused to stir a peg,
Till the lawyers had fasten'd on her Leg,
 As fast as the Law could tie it.

Firmly then—and more firmly yet—
With scorn for scorn, and with threat for threat,
 The Proud One confronted the Cruel:
And loud and bitter the quarrel arose,
Fierce and merciless—one of those,
With spoken daggers, and looks like blows,
 In all but the bloodshed a duel!

AND HER PRECIOUS LEG.

Rash, and wild, and wretched and wrong,
Were the words that came from Weak and Strong,
  Till madden'd for desperate matters;
Fierce as tigress escaped from her den,
She flew to her desk—'twas open'd—and then,
In the time it takes to try a pen,
Or the clerk to utter his slow Amen,

Her Will was in fifty tatters!

But the Count instead of curses wild,
Only nodded his head and smiled,
As if at the spleen of an angry child;
   But the calm was deceitful and sinister!
A lull like the lull of the treacherous sea—
For Hate in that moment had sworn to be
The Golden Leg's sole Legatee,
   And that very night to administer!

Her Death.

'Tis a stern and startling thing to think
How often mortality stands on the brink
   Of its grave without any misgiving:
And yet in this slippery world of strife,
In the stir of human bustle so rife!
There are daily sounds to tell us that Life
   Is dying, and Death is living.

Ay, Beauty the Girl and Love the Boy,
Bright as they are with hope and joy,

AND HER PRECIOUS LEG.

How their souls would sadden instanter,
To remember that one of those wedding bells,
Which ring so merrily through the dells,
   Is the same that knells
     Our last farewells,
Only broken into a canter!

But breath and blood set doom at nought—

MISS KILMANSEGG

How little the wretched Countess thought,
  When at night she unloosed her sandal,
That the Fates had woven her burial-cloth,
And that Death, in the shape of a Death's Head Moth,
  Was fluttering round her candle!

As she look'd at her clock of or-molu,
For the hours she had gone so wearily through
  At the end of a day of trial—
How little she saw in her pride of prime
The dart of Death in the Hand of Time—
  That hand which moved on the dial!

As she went with her taper up the stair,
How little her swollen eye was aware
  That the Shadow that follow'd was double!
Or when she closed her chamber door,
It was shutting out, and for evermore,
  The world—and its worldly trouble.

Little she dreamt, as she laid aside
Her jewels—after one glance of pride—
  They were solemn bequests to Vanity—

AND HER PRECIOUS LEG.

Or when her robes she began to doff,
That she stood so near to the putting off
  Of the flesh that clothes humanity.

And when she quench'd the taper's light,
How little she thought as the smoke took flight
That her day was done—and merged in a night
  Of dreams and duration uncertain—
      Or along with her own,
     That a Hand of Bone
  Was closing mortality's curtain!

But life is sweet, and mortality blind,
And youth is hopeful, and Fate is kind
  In concealing the day of sorrow;
And enough is the present tense of toil—
For this world is, to all, a stiffish soil—
And the mind flies back with a glad recoil
  From the debts not due till to-morrow.

Wherefore else does the Spirit fly
And bid its daily cares good-bye,
  Along with its daily clothing?
Just as the felon condemn'd to die—
  With a very natural loathing—

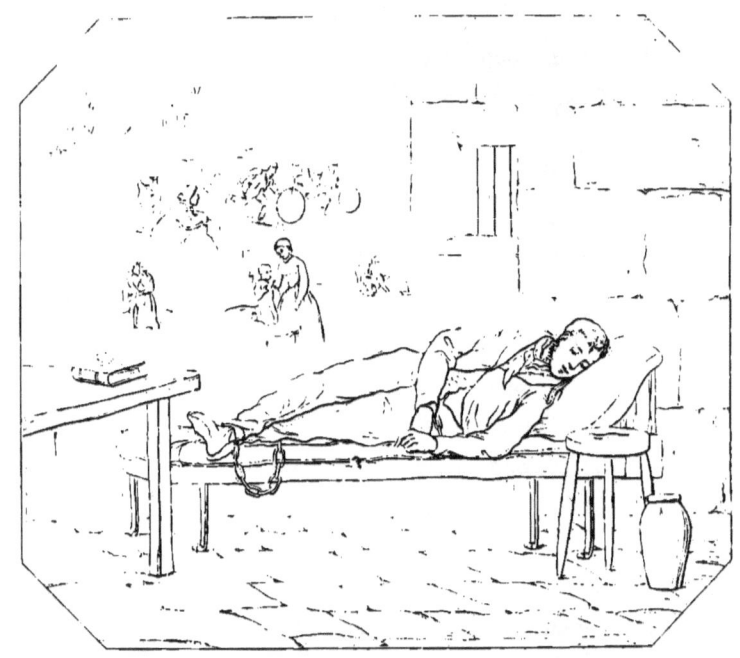

Leaving the Sheriff to dream of ropes,
From his gloomy cell in a vision elopes,
To caper on sunny greens and slopes,
 Instead of the dance upon nothing.

Thus, even thus, the Countess slept,
While Death still nearer and nearer crept,
 Like the Thane who smote the sleeping—
But her mind was busy with early joys,
Her golden treasures and golden toys,
 That flash'd a bright

AND HER PRECIOUS LEG

And golden light
Under lids still red with weeping.

The golden doll that she used to hug!
Her coral of gold, and the golden mug!
Her godfather's golden presents!
The golden service she had at her meals,
The golden watch, and chain, and seals,
Her golden scissors, and thread, and reels,
And her golden fishes and pheasants!

The golden guineas in silken purse—
And the Golden Legends she heard from her nurse,
Of the Mayor in his gilded carriage—
And London streets that were paved with gold—
And the Golden Eggs that were laid of old—
With each golden thing
To the golden ring
At her own auriferous Marriage!

And still the golden light of the sun
Through her golden dream appear'd to run,
Though the night, that roar'd without was one
To terrify seamen or gipsies—
While the moon, as if in malicious mirth,
Kept peeping down at the ruffled earth,
As though she enjoy'd the tempest's birth,
In revenge of her old eclipses.

But vainly, vainly, the thunder fell,
For the soul of the Sleeper was under a spell
  That time had lately embitter'd—
The Count, as once at her foot he knelt—
That foot which now he wanted to melt!
  And some object before her glitter'd.

'Twas the Golden Leg!—she knew its gleam!
And up she started, and tried to scream,—
But—hush!—'twas a stir at her pillow she felt—
  But ev'n in the moment she started—

Down came the limb with a frightful smash,

AND HER PRECIOUS LEG.

And, lost in the universal flash
That her eyeballs made at so mortal a crash,
  The Spark, call'd Vital, departed!

    *   *   *   *   *   *

Gold, still gold! hard, yellow, and cold,
For gold she had lived, and she died for gold
  By a golden weapon—not oaken;
In the morning they found her all alone—
Stiff, and bloody, and cold as stone—
But her Leg, the Golden Leg, was gone,
  And the "Golden Bowl was broken!"

Gold—still gold! it haunted her yet—
At the Golden Lion the Inquest met—
  Its foreman, a carver and gilder—
And the Jury debated from twelve till three
What the Verdict ought to be,
And they brought it in as Felo de Se,
  "Because her own Leg had kill'd her!"

Her Moral.

Gold! Gold! Gold! Gold!
Bright and yellow, hard and cold,
Molten, graven, hammer'd and roll'd;
Heavy to get, and light to hold;
Hoarded, barter'd, bought, and sold,
Stolen, borrow'd, squander'd, doled:
Spurn'd by the young, but hugg'd by the old
To the very verge of the churchyard mould;
Price of many a crime untold;
Gold! Gold! Gold! Gold!
Good or bad a thousand fold!
   How widely its agencies vary—
To save—to ruin—to curse—to bless—
As even its minted coins express,
Now stamp'd with the image of GOOD QUEEN BESS
   And now of a BLOODY MARY.

Works published by Moxon, Son, & Co.

Cloth, gilt edges, Eight Illustrations, price 3s. 6d. each.

MOXON'S POPULAR POETS.
Edited by WILLIAM MICHAEL ROSSETTI.

The press and the public, alike in Great Britain and her Colonies, and in the United States, unite in their testimony to the immense superiority of Messrs. Moxon's Popular Poets, over any other similar collections published by any other house. Their possession of the copyright works of Coleridge, Hood, Keats, Shelley, Wordsworth, and other great national poets, places this series above rivalry. Upwards of 100,000 volumes have already been sold.

Tupper's Proverbial Philosophy in this Series is expected to have an enormous sale.

BYRON'S POETICAL WORKS.
LONGFELLOW'S POETICAL WORKS.
WORDSWORTH'S POETICAL WORKS.
SCOTT'S POETICAL WORKS.
SHELLEY'S POETICAL WORKS.
MOORE'S POETICAL WORKS.
HOOD'S POETICAL WORKS.
KEATS' POETICAL WORKS.
COLERIDGE'S POETICAL WORKS.
BURNS' POETICAL WORKS.
TUPPER'S PROVERBIAL PHILOSOPHY.
The Four Series complete for the first time in 1 Vol., with Portrait.
MILTON'S POETICAL WORKS.
CAMPBELL'S POETICAL WORKS.
COWPER'S POETICAL WORKS. *[Shortly.*
POPE'S POETIAL WORKS. *[Shortly.*
LYRA ELEGANTIARUM:

Any of Moxon's Popular Poets in morocco, plain, 10s. 6d.; ditto, antique, 7s. 6d.; ivory enamel, 6s. 6d.; suitable for Christmas presents.

The Haydn's Series of Manuals.
Price 18s. *cloth,* 21s. *half-calf,* 24s. *calf,* 32s. *morocco.*

Haydn's Dictionary of Dates.
RELATING TO ALL AGES AND NATIONS; FOR UNIVERSAL REFERENCE: 13th Edition, with Supplement bringing the history of the world down to the end of 1870.

Price 18s. *cloth,* 21s. *half-calf,* 24s. *calf,* 32s. *morocco.*
Haydn's Universal Index of Biography.
FROM THE CREATION TO THE PRESENT TIME. For the use of the Statesman, the Historian, and the Journalist. Containing the chief events in the lives of eminent persons of all ages and nations, arranged chronologically and carefully dated; preceded by the Biographies and Genealogies of the chief Royal Houses of the world.

Price 18s. *cloth,* 21s. *half-calf,* 24s. *calf,* 32s. *morocco.*
Haydn's Dictionary of Science.
Comprising Astronomy, Chemistry, Dynamics, Electricity, Heat, Hydrodynamics, Hydrostatics, Light, Magnetism, Mechanics, Meteorology, Pneumatics, Sound and Statics; preceded by an essay on the History of the Physical Sciences.

Price 18s. *cloth,* 21s. *half-calf,* 24s. *calf,* 32s. *morocco.*
Haydn's Dictionary of the Bible.
For the Use of all Readers and Students of the Holy Scriptures of the Old and New Testaments, and of the Books of the Apocrypha.

LONDON: E. MOXON, SON, & CO., DOVER STREET, W.,
AND 1, AMEN CORNER, E.C.

www.ingramcontent.com/pod-product-compliance
Lightning Source LLC
Chambersburg PA
CBHW030317170426
43202CB00009B/1035